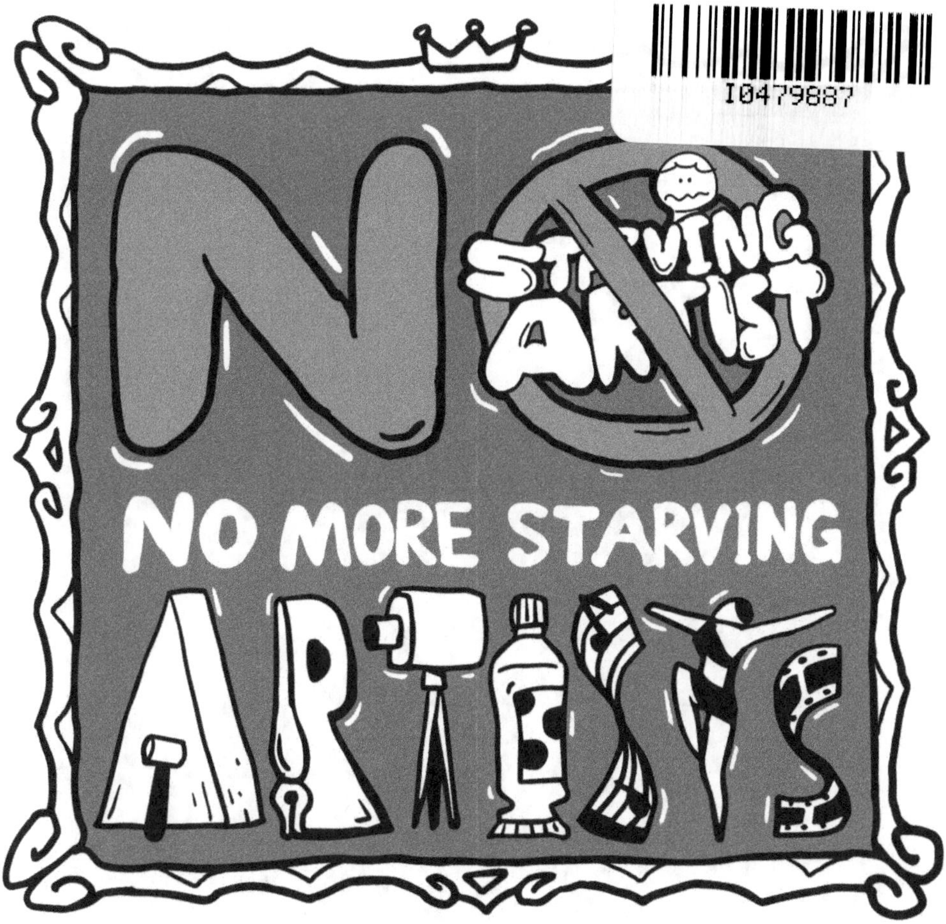

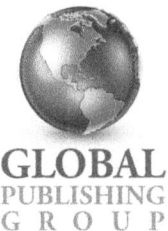

Global Publishing Group
Australia • New Zealand • Singapore • America • London

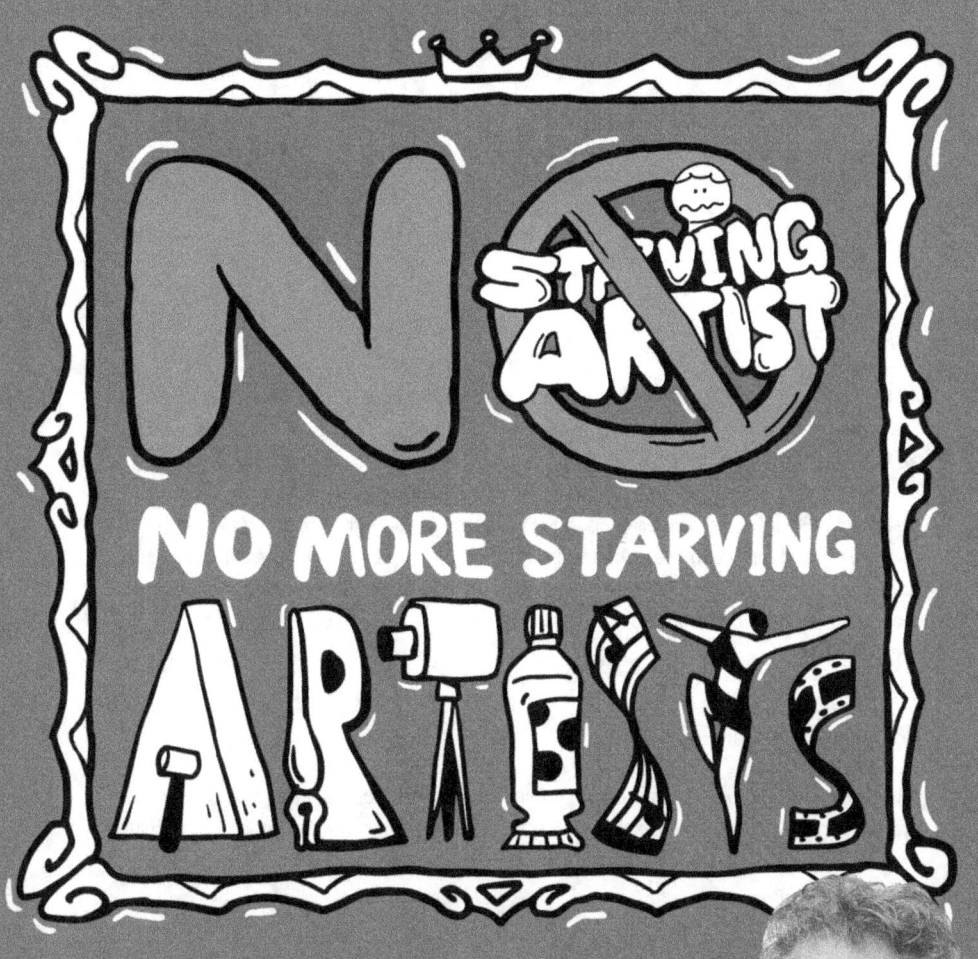

NO MORE STARVING ARTISTS

How to Master Your Art, Your Life & Build Your Business

"The world needs more successful and sane artists"

FOREWORD BY AMANDA PALMER

JOHN PAUL FISCHBACH

A catalogue record for this book is available from the National Library of Australia

Published by Global Publishing Group
PO Box 517 Mt Evelyn, Victoria 3796 Australia
Email info@GlobalPublishingGroup.com.au

Printed in USA

For further information about orders:
Phone: +61 3 9739 4686 or Fax +61 3 8648 6871

I dedicate this book to every artist who chooses a life that is rewarding, challenging and difficult to explain.

To every artist who opens hearts, stretches minds and changes lives with your art.

To Craig Lambie, Alia Vryens, Julie-Anne Black and Clarice Evans whose belief in me and the work of the Auspicious Arts Incubator has transformed the lives of artists around the world.

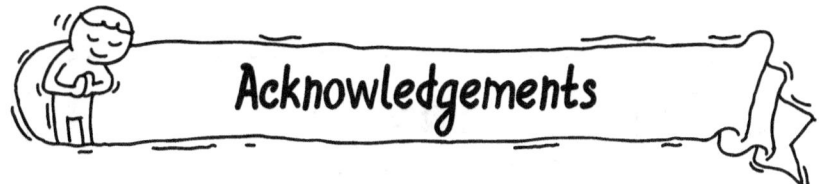

Acknowledgements

It has been an honour and a privilege to write this book. As with any major project, there are a number of very special people who contributed to making this book happen. I'd like to take this opportunity to say, "Thank you."

A special thank you to the core team members who have joined me on this mission to help artists. John Paxinos, Craig Lambie, Benno Rentinck, Deirdre O'Brien, Aneke McCulloch, Peta Hanrahan, Phil Evans, Mark Crees, Ros Walker, Selene Bateman, Alia Vryens, Julie-Anne Black, Liz O'Brien, Alan Kiff, Gavin John, Lendl Macapinlac, Laura Gonzalez, Lester Perez, Tessa Pope, Fred Chuang, Bohao, Maree Cohen, Callum Fox.

There have been so many mentors, guides, colleagues, and friends who have taught me, supported me, and inspired me along the way. Linda Fleet, Georgie Davill, Rod Ainsworth, Liz Zito, Rebecca Cherry, Peter Tullin, Suzanne Daley, Sue Hunt, Candace Sorensen, Rebecca Coleman, Heather Potinio, Margaret Hunt, Jesse Elliott, Angie Kim, Alan Brown, Randi Burns, Wendy Holmes, Douglas Riske, Madeline King, Druh Farrell, Tracey Read, Robert Bush, Kelly Barsdate, Gary Steuer, Sharon Louden, Ruby Learner, Allyson McGrane, Tracey Read, Lesley Cook, Dorelle Peters, Peter Wohelski, Jesse Stanley, Victoria Templeton, Sanda Aye, Sharon Davis, Christopher Howard, Scott James Hayward, Susan Guggenheim, Calvin Coyles, Marie Budimir, Emily Fletcher, T Harv Eker, Brendon Burchard, Marissa Peer, Tellman Knudson, Bill Baren, Ian Spicer, Rick Schnabel, Sai Blackbyrn, Chloe Beevers, Yamile Yemoonyah.

Andrea Lemon, Andrea Rieniets, and the hundreds of artists who have been part of our programs and courses and all the presenters of Secret of Success seminars. You have inspired me and proven that we can bust the myth of the Starving Artist.

This book would never have happened without the expert guidance of Darren Stephens, Kelly Mayne, the team at Global Publishing Group, and the expert eye of Aaron Murphy and the PaperTrue team.

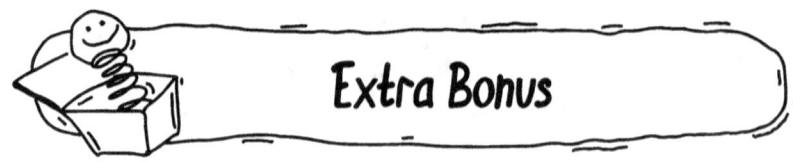

Extra Bonus

I can't give you absolutely everything you need to know about busting
the myth of the Starving Artist in this one small book.

You'll find lots more support and help designed specifically for artists at

www.auspiciousartsincubator.org

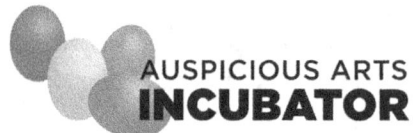

As a special bonus for you, I'd like to welcome you into the Auspicious
Successful Artists Program, ASAP, an exclusive membership site for
artists in business.

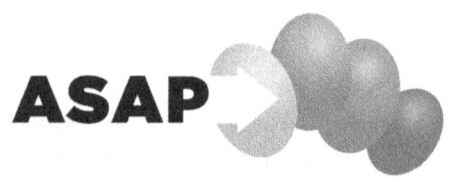

Your first month is free when you use this link:

www.aai.guru/asapfree

Table of Contents

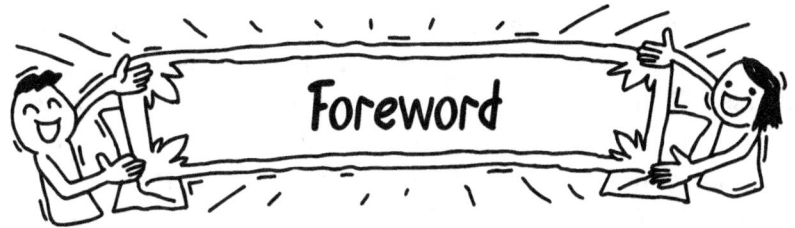

Hello, creator of Things! I'd like to start off by congratulating you for picking up this book and investing your time and energy in the admittedly annoying, yet essential task of grappling with the 'business' side of your art. Your nightmares may be about to end!

John Paul has taken his hard-won knowledge of how best to help independent artists and combined it with over a decade of experience helping artists in Australia, Canada and the US. He's here to help, and there's lots of gems for you to discover, mull, and take out into the field with you as you head back into the wide world of creating. Use the parts of the book that fit, skip the ones that don't apply. And for heaven's sake: stop trying to do it all by yourself. Stop over-apologizing, stop fretting, stop justifying and for god's sake . . . just ask. The help you need might be staring you right in the face.

You may finally be able to get your shit together! It is time to celebrate, because the contents of this book are the nightmare-stuffs of almost every artist I know, and for so many reasons: it isn't sexy, it isn't romantic, it isn't 'artistic', and, in some of our twisted art-brains, it's downright 'inauthentic' to think practically about the business side of art. Well, I call bullshit on that. The most authentic gift you can give your creation is the loving, caring time and attention to make sure it's passage into the world, and into other hands, is a safe and fair one. This book is a great primer and resource for any artist interested in getting their hands enjoyably dirty in the garden where art and business entangle with one another.

My journey to finally making a living from my art was similar to so many other musicians and painters and writers: I waded my way through an eclectic array of odd jobs and terrible gigs and random opportunities to eventually land the success and freedom I enjoy today, and I still work my ass off on a daily basis, doing tons of things I'd rather not be doing: ticking off annoying, endless lists of administrative tasks and despairing that my email inbox will never be empty (hint: it's not). Every day I close my laptop and know that I didn't get it all done, and I forgive myself, and I start again on the pile of endlessness in the morning. Every day I try not to beat myself up about the art-life balance that I feel I am continually failing to achieve. And every day I get better at reminding myself that even though I never got through the list, and I didn't strike the right balance, it's okay; I did Enough. As long as you keep showing up at the desk, at the easel, at the pottery wheel, at the laptop, you're already halfway there. Nobody is there to applaud you at the end of a long day of sending out packages, but you can also rest easy in the knowledge that no great artist ever rolled out of bed and got handed a gold star for being a genius. Every successful artist I know spends an inordinate amount of time on un-sexy business and irritating tasks, and the less shame and guilt they feel about it, the more time they have to devote to their craft with a clear head.

The world needs more successful and sane artists, not more struggling and unhinged artists. Artists are unhinged enough to begin with (why else would we go into the arts?) and the cultural baggage and expectations from the world - that we're incapable of sorting out our affairs - is a poisonous one. The romantic notion that artists should stay up in the freezing garret, painting their sorrowful masterpieces and subsisting on cigarettes and red wine while everybody else down in the town square gets on with the hustle-bustle of ordinary exchange, eating actual food, is not only stupid, it's dangerous. Artists who buy into the romantic starving artist stereotype are not only doing themselves a disservice, they're doing a disservice to the world, because nobody can contribute beautiful, meaningful, and thought-provoking art to the community when you're collapsed on an attic floor due to liver failure.

Meanwhile, the world of the internet has levelled the playing field and made it possible for all artists to share their art with anybody around the globe, but it's also destroyed our privacy and boundaries. We can lie there in bed for hours, flipping through screens, trying to make progress, trying to get people to like us, trying to find like-minded souls, trying, trying, trying to connect our soul to the other souls in the darkness in a never-ending bid to make more progress. But we can forget, sometimes, that giving our poor brains a break from constantly connecting and promoting can also be the key to letting our creative minds take over the wheel. Without that time to let our inner artists drive the car, we run out of gas, and then there's nothing worth sharing to begin with. Don't forget to switch that shit off every once in a while, and this is coming from a full-time internet addict.

Part of my mission - and this was such a passion for me that I did a TED talk and wrote a book called "The Art of Asking" - is to tell my artist friends that it is OKAY TO ASK for things, and it is OKAY TO SAY YES TO HELP. There's no award given for those artists who made it to the top with the least support. In fact, it's the support that infuses your life with balance, with connection, with the reminder that we're all interwoven; a reminder that this life isn't a question of winning, succeeding, and getting to the top of the mountain first. It's about being together. Connecting through art, through song, through stories. The very things that make us human, that make life worth living in the first place. So remember, my fellow artists: It is okay to ask for money, and it is okay to ask for help. If art really is your contribution to the tribe, then it has a value to the world, even if that value is only treasured by a small community of people. Not everything is, nor should be, blockbuster-level. Appreciate your tribe, and the support they try to give. That's what making art for each other is all about.

It's a crazy place, but it's totally possible to navigate, and you've already started by flipping this book open. John Paul is gonna hold your hand.

Amanda Palmer
Woodstock, NY
December 2017

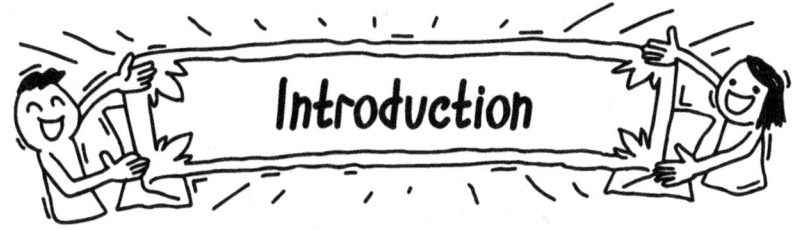

Thank you for choosing a life that is hard from time to time, but also joyous and somewhat difficult to explain. This book has been written for you and all independent artists who have made the empowering choice of using your creative talent, to live a life full of passion and to be the authors of your own destiny. When you set out to live your life as an artist, no one told you that you needed a whole bunch of other skills to complement your artistic talent. If you want to succeed in business as an artist and make a living from your awesome talent, some basic skills, once you acquire them, will keep you from living on the brink of poverty. Artists need help to learn marketing and sales, time management, bookkeeping, and some of the 88 other skills that it takes to run a successful small arts business.

I can hear some of you say, "Whoa, wait, all I wanna do is make art!" And so you should. And so you will. You are unique. You have been given a special talent. You have developed your talent. You have developed your talent through hard work and practice. You have the innate ability to imagine something never seen before, amazing skills to manifest your visions, and a seemingly inexhaustible supply of creative ideas. But as you know by now, artistic talent ≠ business talent. But hey, it's the 21st century. You can leverage your talent and your creativity and create a fantastic business that will let you mould your career around your artistic lifestyle. This book is for you and for all independent artists who have realised that you are also small business operators, and that there are some marketing and business skills that you need to get a handle on in order to live the life you want to live.

In my own journey as an independent artist, I realised very quickly that I was a small business operator. I was that little kid who got all the neighbourhood kids to come together, develop an original show, rehearse it, and perform it in the living room. The difference was that I thought of it as a business, and I charged everyone a quarter to watch the show.

OK, so who am I and why should you be listening to me? Well, I was once a struggling artist too.

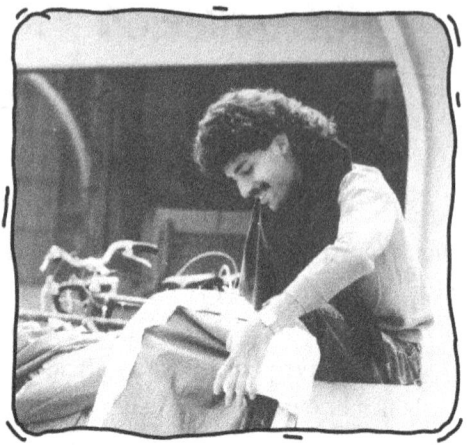

That's a picture of me fresh out of University, after receiving my Master of Fine Arts degree in Directing. I created a travelling stilt company. And yes, we've all had hairstyles that we wish had not been photographed.

I discovered the magic of theatre as a kid, and I knew that I wanted to create that magic for the enjoyment of others. For me, my work has always been about the audience's enjoyment. I got my grade two class to put on little plays and tour them to the other classrooms. (Honestly, I did that.) By grade eight, I had formed a touring troop called "The Fun Company" that took shows to hospitals. I continue to work as a serial entrepreneur to this very day.

I also went to very prestigious schools and studied with some of the great masters of theatre: Joseph Chaikin, Jerzy Grotowski, Betsy Shevey, to name a few. I finally completed my Master of Fine Arts degree in Directing from the University of Alberta. And there I was: a highly skilled and talented director of theatre, opera, musicals, and avant-garde physical performance work, ready to set sail.

I flung myself out into the world. I was hired by theatre companies, opera companies and festivals. But by far, the most rewarding experiences I had were the times when I got to create original works, start new festivals, start new theatre companies, start new tours or open new galleries, because this fed my soul as both an artist and an entrepreneur.

INTRODUCTION

I've worked on both big productions and small. I've been a producer of the Olympic Arts Festival with a budget of millions, and I've been the founding artistic director of a shamanic theatre company in the Rocky Mountains, with a budget limited to the credit on my Visa card. I've converted warehouses into galleries and performance spaces in the US, the UK, Canada, and Australia. I've also helped raise millions of dollars to build a performing arts centre in Calgary.

After ten years as the founding artistic director of Vertigo Theatre in Calgary, I decided I needed a break, and I set sail once again. I took a year off to recharge my creative batteries and travel the world. Along the journey, I arrived in Melbourne, Australia. I was blown away by the creativity, and so I stayed. As I looked around at the dynamic independent art scene, I was saddened to observe that these vibrant awesome artistic businesses were able to last only about three to five years. Artists were throwing in the towel not because their art sucked, but because they couldn't make their artistic practice succeed as a business. As you well know, you can only live off the smell of an oily rag for so long. Eventually you want to buy a car or a house, you want to get married, you want to start a family. So here I was in Melbourne, where there were artists doing great work but giving up way too soon. They needed business and marketing skills to thrive.

I realised that I could help. I created Australia's only incorporated, not-for-profit, social enterprise business arts incubator, dedicated to helping build sustainable creative businesses by giving independent artists and small to medium arts organisations the business and marketing skills, along with the confidence, they need to thrive. And I'm proud to say that, ten years later, I've been able to make a significant difference. We've helped thousands of artists to get their marketing and business shit together. We have helped guarantee a future for hundreds of vibrant sustainable arts businesses in a huge range of arts practice: visual arts disciplines, theatre, dance, music, community cultural development, film, and gaming. My coaching team and I have transformed the lives and careers of fine artists, jewellers, actors, dancers, poets, choreographers, directors, sculptors, photographers, writers, illustrators, painters, visual artists, composers, musicians, singers, multimedia artists, filmmakers, animators, game designers, and community arts facilitators. So, I'm pretty confident that this book can help you too.

NOTE: The spelling in this book is Australian. I've written this book while living in Australia, and the publisher is based in Australia, so I've used Australian spellings. Down under, we use the spellings 'colour' and 'organisation' and 'favour.'

And that brings me to the present. I am and continue to be a working, practicing, independent artist. I've created books, films, audio theatre mobile phone apps, a web series, and still direct the occasional opera and play. My life is a balance of creating independent art, growing several arts businesses, and helping my fellow artists. But there's more to my story as a successful independent artist.

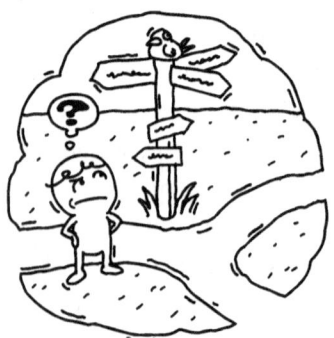

There are three plot twists to my story. The first one came on the eve of my 27th birthday. Now, for those of you who might not know this, your 27th birthday is a significant one because, astrologically speaking, it's your Saturn return, and that means it's a time when your soul seeks to find its true purpose and many people's lives take a new direction.

Well, in my case, my soul was seeking its spiritual path and I found myself apprenticed to a medicine woman. This started me down a new path of traditional Native American and Native Canadian shamanic training. I emerged as a site whisperer, and a ceremony man. Well, since that time, the spiritual side of my artistic practice has grown to the point where I can no longer distinguish the edges between art and shamanism, but that's a whole different story. Becoming a shaman was the first plot twist.

The second plot twist happened about three years later, when I realised that as a director/producer, I was starting and running small businesses, and I was lacking some fundamental business and marketing skills. I was 'livin' the dream'. I was artistically and spiritually fulfilled, but most of the time I was broke. When this this plot twist occurred, I happened to be working at the Banff Centre for the Arts in the New Music Theatre program. We got a visit from the vice president of the Centre for Management. He told us that he was being asked by top CEOs and clients to teach them how to be creative and innovative and able to deal with change. The VP of the Centre wasn't sure how to do that. He wondered if we could help. I said, "Sure, I'll give it a try." And for two and a half years, I had the great good fortune of helping teach creativity to top CEOs. But at the same time, I got to be in the classroom and hear incredible instructors teach CEOs the keys to business, the secrets of successful leadership, marketing, HR, strategic planning, and business planning. I soaked it all up. For two and a half years, I got an education in business. And I've continued learning ever since.

I would estimate that I have invested several hundreds of thousands of dollars on my education since I graduated with my Master of Fine Arts degree. I've taken courses, attended seminars, hired coaches, joined master mind groups and read hundreds of books. For me, if I'm not learning, I'm not growing.

That opportunity at the Banff Centre showed me that I was a serial entrepreneur. It taught me what I needed to learn about business and leadership. And you can rest assured that the next arts businesses I created were a lot more financially successful than the first ones.

That brings us to the third plot twist in the story of my life. After arriving in Melbourne, I realised that if I was going to help other artists with my arts incubator business, I needed to acquire yet more new skills. The thing that holds so many artists back is a limiting belief, or a lack of confidence, or some negative self-talk. If I was going to truly help artists transform their lives and their careers, I needed to learn to help artists manage their minds and their emotions.

I set myself on a four-year journey of discovery. I investigated every self-help mind and emotion management tool I could find. I became a certified NLP (Neuro-Linguistic Programming) practitioner and helped artists change behaviour. I became trained in the Reconnection and helped artists upgrade their operating systems. I learned PSYCH-K and helped artists install powerful positive beliefs directly into their subconscious. I became an Ericksonian hypnotherapist and a certified life coach, all in the spirit of helping artists and myself to be masters of our minds and our emotions.

There is a bigger reason for why we do what we do at the Auspicious Arts Incubator.

I value artists, because I am one myself. We are the people who stretch minds, open hearts, and change lives. I believe that we, the artists of the world, are our most valuable citizens.

Welcome to this book. My hope is that it ignites within you a burning desire to want more, to do more, and to learn more. I don't want the world to lose a single one of you because you don't have the business and marketing skills you need to succeed. Your talent is a gift that is needed right now. The world is potentially sliding into a very dangerous place, and it is going to be us, the artists, who turn things around and bring the world into balance. The world can't afford to lose you. You need to become a powerful force of good and love and beauty and vision and change…so let's get cracking!

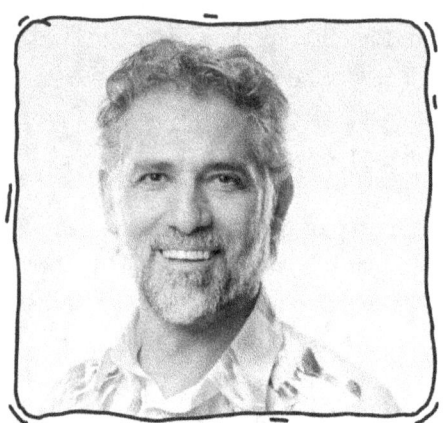

 www.AuspiciousArtsIncubator.org

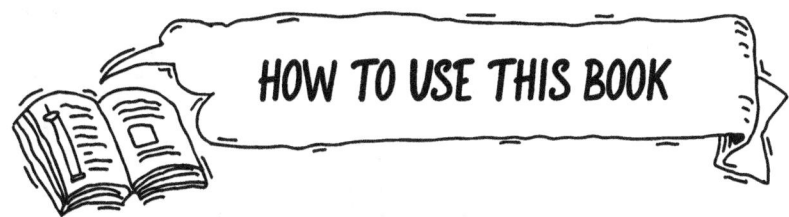

HOW TO USE THIS BOOK

This book is divided into five sections. After being educated by the best of the best in business and leadership and starting so many arts businesses, I've come to realise that there are five fundamentals of a successful small arts business. It's something that artists are never taught. I call these 'The Five Pillars of Your Successful Arts Business.'

I've had the privilege of collaborating with an awesome freelance illustrator to create this book. Bohao and I created these two images to help you visualise your journey through this book. Every one of you have created a unique and interesting arts business.

Your amazing business is currently in danger of collapsing due to the weak foundation pillars supporting your world.

This book will help you create five solid pillars to support your arts business and make it sustainable.

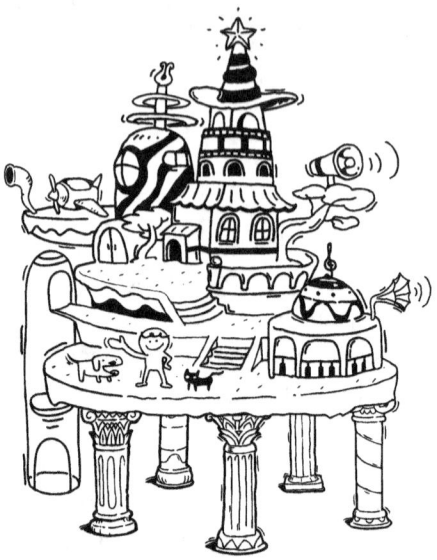

The first three pillars help you, the business owner, to clarify what your unique arts business is about. Each one gets you clear about your art becoming your business.

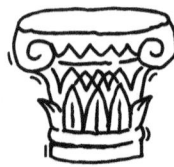

Pillar 1: Vision & Mindset

What does your version of success look like?
Do you believe you can and will succeed?

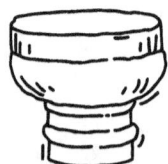

Pillar 2: Branding & Values

Why are you doing this? How do you stay true to what's important to you?

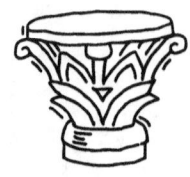

Pillar 3: Marketing & Message

Who are your customers? Why do they want you, and what you have to offer?

The next two pillars comprise the skills you need as the CEO of your arts business.

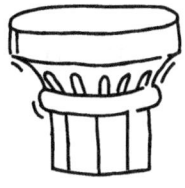

Pillar 4: Money & Finance

How to manage your money and get comfortable seeing your art from the perspective of numbers.

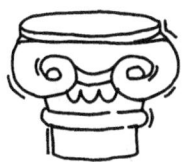

Pillar 5: Planning & Productivity

How to grow your business and manage it all so that you don't burn out.

You build or re-engineer your arts business by erecting these five pillars in this order. You develop your vision and your mindset first. These two skills elements are critical for artists to be able to build your unique and successful small business. You must be able to construct a vision of where you're going, and you must have the right mindset to believe that you'll get there.

Once you've got that down, you need to develop your brand by communicating with your fans, followers, customers, and your audience to find out what they say about you and your art. You need to align their description of you with your values. You want to make sure that your business is delivering benefits, solving problems, and helping others in ways that are important to you and to them.

And then, if you know where you're heading, and your customers want you and what you have to offer, it's time to work on finding more customers and growing your market. That boils down to learning about marketing and using value-based language to deliver your unique message of value and impact. Once you've got those three pillars in place, you have a viable business. You have steady money coming in from your products and services and money going out to create your art and grow your business.

Now it's time to learn to manage all this money and educate yourself about the financial side of your arts business. You need this fourth pillar because you can't manage what you can't measure. Every small business owner (artists included) must be able to understand, measure, and manage their money.

The more you learn and grow, the bigger your business gets. Your market expands, and the value of what you produce increases. More money starts to come into the business, and more business means longer hours and more work. But you don't want to burn out. It's time for the fifth and final pillar of planning and productivity. You must make plans, set goals, measure progress, and make course corrections when necessary. It is essential at this stage to learn to manage your time and build a team around you.

If you jump around in this book, looking at the chapters that you feel are urgent, you'll build an interesting business, but you're likely to burn out too quickly because the success that you experience will be sporadic. Your success won't be managed, and worst of all, it won't be built on a solid foundation of these five pillars. You won't be able to support the growth of your business.

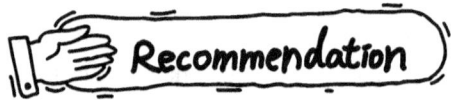

Read this book with a friend. Like many things in life, it's more fun in a group. One of the best guarantees of your success is to find an accountability buddy: someone who will hold you accountable for making it through each of these pillars. If you team up with another artist, you will 10X the growth of your arts business.

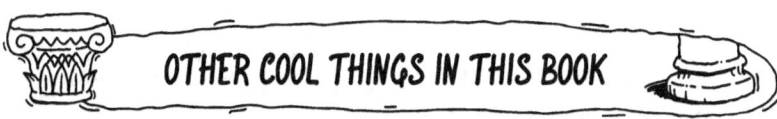

OTHER COOL THINGS IN THIS BOOK

There are **practical exercises** throughout this book.

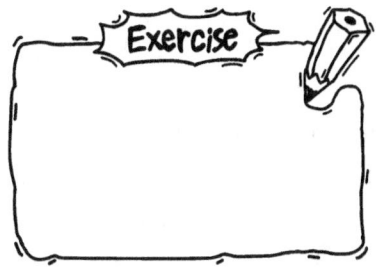

I highly recommend that you actually pause your reading and do them right then. As artists, we learn best when we physically do what we've just learned. The exercises I've included in this book are designed for you to execute at the very moment you read them. They are not academic cerebral activities—they are practical, and have already helped hundreds of artists get ahead. But these exercises are only a starting place. When you work with us in any of our programs, there are many more exercises and much more knowledge that we give you to guarantee your proficiency in each of these five pillars.

There are **Secrets of Success** peppered through-out the book. These secrets are the 'aha' moments, when artists who have worked with us have said, "Wow, I wish someone had told me that a year ago." So, I'm sharing those moments with you now. When you see one of these (see right), pause and reflect how it might apply to you. Quite possibly, it's something you need to know, accept, adopt, or understand. Apply the concept to yourself and your arts business.

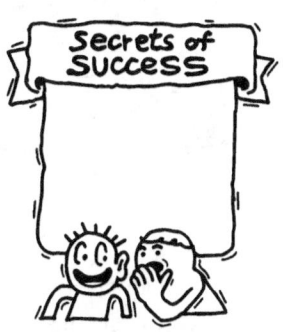

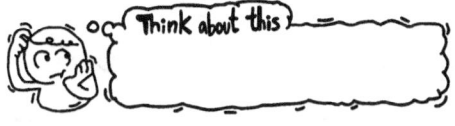

Sometimes there are things that you should think about that will change your perception. I offer these tips for mindset adjustment throughout the book.

There are also **Stories of Success**. These are case studies of artists who have successfully built 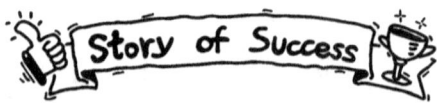 the Five Pillars. All the things in this book work when you apply them. I want you to meet a handful of artists who have a burning desire to commit themselves to building their arts businesses. They were all willing to invest their time and their money to learn everything there is to learn to make their business succeed.

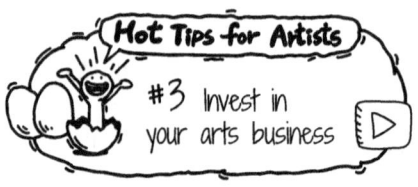

There are also some bonus links to **Hot Tips for Artists** video blog posts. At certain points as I was writing this book, I thought, "I wish they could just watch the Hot Tip video on this." When you see this image, you can go to our website or to YouTube and check out that particular Hot Tip.

This book has been designed to help improve your existing arts business or perhaps to help you start the journey of building your arts business. It's also a good resource for information and motivation you can share with other artists.

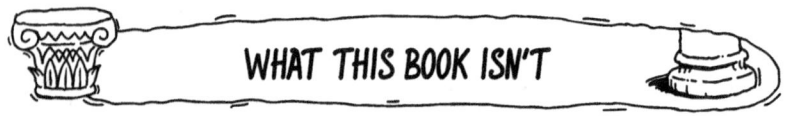

WHAT THIS BOOK ISN'T

This book is not a magic bullet.

This book can't possibly give you everything you need to know. There are 92 discrete skills required to run a successful small arts business. For this to be a comprehensive text, it would need to comprise at least 12 volumes and well over 1,500 pages, and I know you wouldn't read that.

This book is not a replacement for our more intensive programs.

If you are like most artist entrepreneurs, at some point you need a disciplined, structured program to make faster, more substantial changes to your arts business. That's why we have created the **Artists Transformations School**, the **Artist's Mojo**, and our other programs and courses.

HOW TO USE THIS BOOK

This book is not a replacement for coaching.

The number one thing that moved my arts businesses to success was working with a coach. Athletes and classical musicians have coaches. We know from those disciplines how valuable a coach is and how a coach can help improve performance. However, independent artists rarely take on a coach to help grow their business. I find this odd. Many small businesses and entrepreneurs use coaches. Perhaps the reason we don't use coaching help is that we don't think of it, and there aren't very many arts business coaches. The external perspective of a trained arts business coach is invaluable for helping you navigate the specific hurdles that inevitably arise along the journey of building your arts business.

This book is not the end of your learning curve.

This book is not the only thing you need to do to succeed. It is intended to give you the basics and help you identify what you need to learn. This book will give you a framework, then it's up to you to seek out the further skills and knowledge you'll need to grow your unique arts business.

Head out on this journey of improving or building your arts business and ending the tradition of the Starving Artist. It's only a matter of mastering your art, your life, and then building a business. Simple, right?

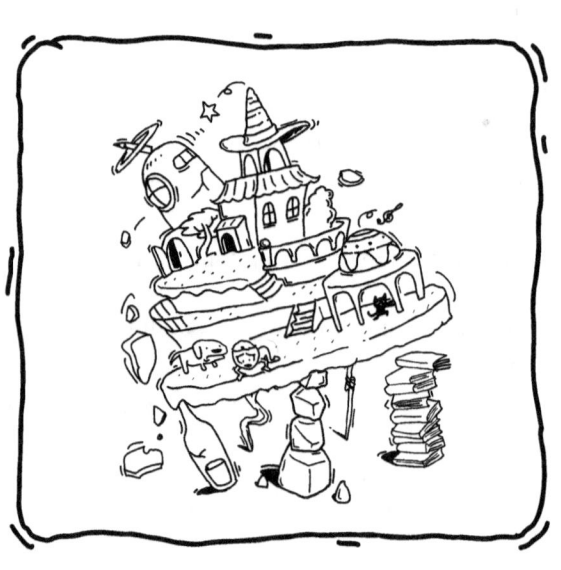

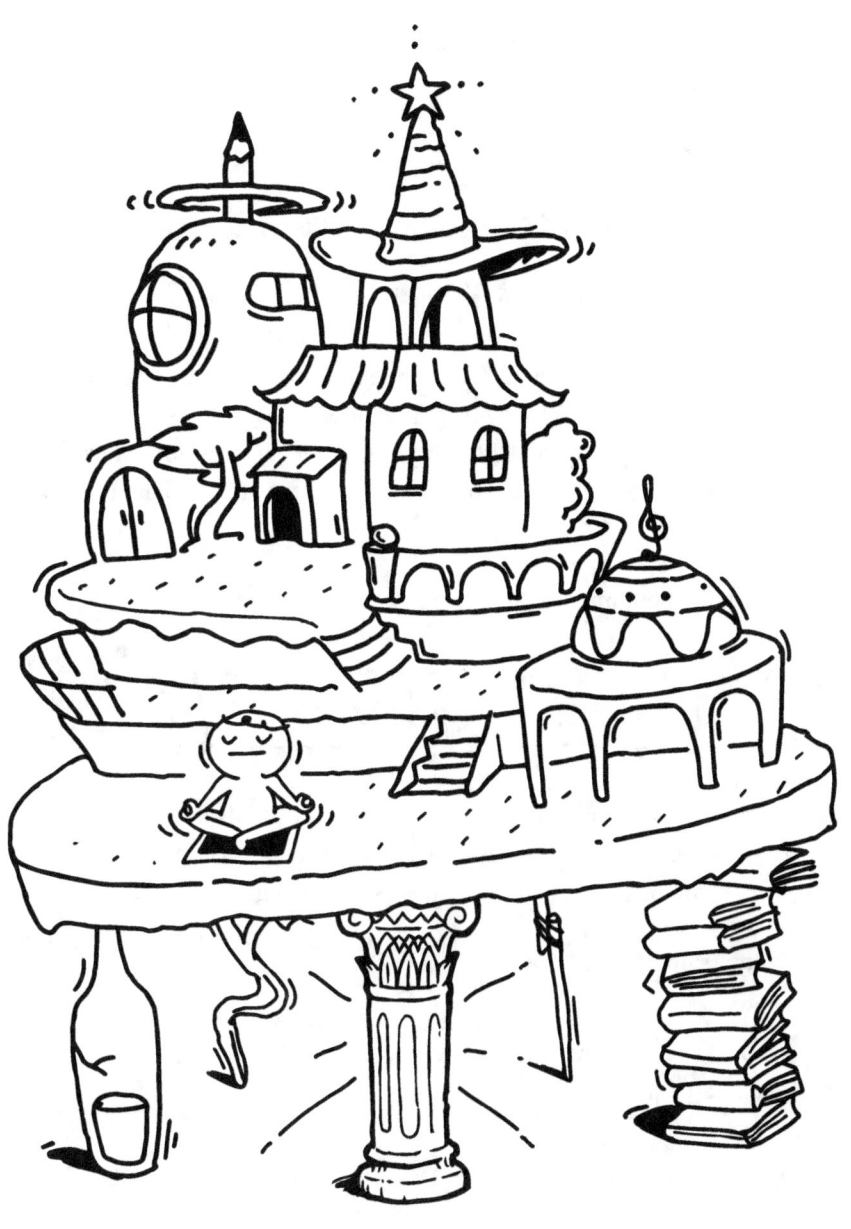

Part 1 Vision & Mindset

This is part one, Vision and Mindset. This part asks you to answer some fundamental questions.

What does your unique version of success look like? Do you believe that you can and will succeed?

This first section is about two things: your Vision and your Mindset. When we talk about vision, we mean, "Where are you heading?" Every artist is unique. Every artistic talent is unique. Your version of your successful business is your own. Where will you be living? How often will you be working? How big is this business going to be? What products or services do you provide? Your unique answers to those questions are all the things that form your vision.

When we talk about mindset, you need to realise that

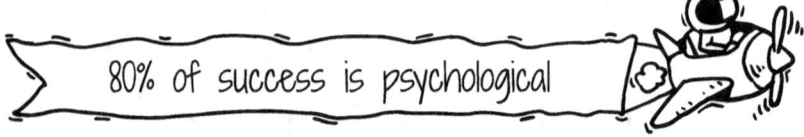

80% of success is psychological

Now in the arts, we tend to believe that 80% of success is due to your talent. But it's not true. In an arts business, 80% of your success is psychological. So I ask you, "Do you have the mindset that is going to get you there?"

Henry Ford said,

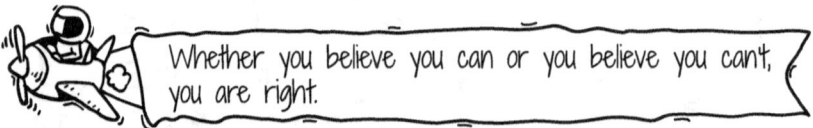

Whether you believe you can or you believe you can't, you are right.

Think about that. It's absolutely true. The artists who believe they can achieve success, do. The artists who believe they can't succeed continue to flounder. On the journey to success, it is not about your resources, it is about your resourcefulness. If you believe you can, you will. Erecting the first pillar for a successful arts business requires you to develop your vision and your mindset. You must get this first one right—that's why it is the first one. It's incredibly critical for all artists (including you) to know where you're going, PLUS you must believe that you will get there.

In this first section, we are going to examine a few skills to master as you develop the vision and mindset of your successful small business. There's a ton of stuff related to ideas in this section. I encourage you to learn as much as you can on the topic of vision and mindset. Everything you master in this area has a flow-on effect to every other part of your business.

I want you to think about a couple of things.

Number 1. I want you to consider that, as artists, we create products and services that other people value.

We have a gift and people value that gift. People receive a benefit from what we create. I want you to consider the fact that these benefits are so valuable that people are willing to give their time and money for them. As a business owner, you want to realise that other people want to gather your wisdom, own some of your creativity, and learn from you and your gift.

Number 2. I would like you to believe that you are powerful.

You are not only talented, you are actually powerful. I would like you to own this, 'artists are cool'. We are interesting. We are exciting. We are exotic. We're mysterious. We are the tall poppies.

Number 3. Lastly, I want you to acknowledge that you have chosen to make your art your life.

And that's a bold choice. Other people hold you in high regard for doing what you love and are envious that you're making a living doing what you love.

Let's dive in and construct a powerful, tall, and strong first pillar. Let's clarify your vision and develop your mindset.

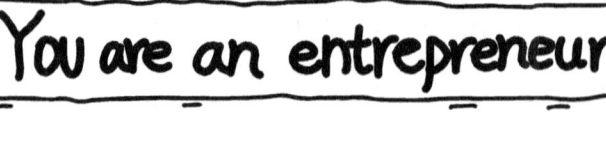

You are an entrepreneur

Artists are natural entrepreneurs. Remember the story I shared with you in the introduction? I was that kid who created original shows in the basement. I recruited the talent. I got the sets built. I gathered the audience. I organised the rehearsals for actors and musicians. And to this day, I do that. I have a vision and I manifest it…over and over. And I bet you do, too. You manifest visions. You reach into the great universal void and see an idea for something that never existed before. And you pull it from that formless place of creative ideas and bring it down to earth. You manifest it, and you build it in 3D here on this physical plane. That act of creation is powerful—not everybody can do that. Not everybody can imagine something, and honestly, not everybody can manifest what they imagine. You see an opportunity and you gather all the resources necessary for producing that unique product or service. That's what an entrepreneur does. They see an opportunity and they manifest it. That's what you do too.

All entrepreneurs leave their comfort zone when they take action. And most importantly, all entrepreneurs stay in action. They do not succumb to the safe and comfortable desire for sitting on the couch eating a tub of ice cream, thinking up cool ideas and saying to themselves, "I'll do that later." Another reason this is a secret of success is that **all change happens outside your comfort zone**.

Secrets of Success

You have to leave your comfort zone, take action and stay in action.

By definition, your comfort zone is the place where you are comfortable, where no change happens, where everything stays the same. There's a part of your brain charged with preserving your comfort zone called the amygdala. Its job is to monitor and preserve the comfort zone so that you are safe and content. The minute that you're trying to do something different, you're trying to grow, you're trying to stretch, you're moving outside your comfort zone. The amygdala immediately wakes up and raises the alarm bell. It says, "Oh my God, what are you doing? We have to stop this! You've never done this before, you must stop! Pull the plug! You can't do this!" Well, that's not helpful when we want to grow and learn and change.

You need to be the boss of your amygdala. Listen to it and say, "Thank you for sounding the alarm. I hear you. I realise that you are just trying to keep me content and comfortable, but I'm handling this. I've got this under control. We're going to be okay. I'm the boss and I'm moving us outside our comfort zone because this is something I want." And the amygdala goes, "Whew, okay, if you really want this, go ahead, but it's way outside the comfort zone."

Here's a mental shift that will take many of you out of your comfort zone.

You used to be an opportunity-seeking missile. You used to put your head up and look around for an opportunity, a call for artists, an audition, a request for proposals, and you would seize that opportunity. Well, what I want you to do now is to move from being an opportunity-seeking missile to becoming an opportunity creator. I want you I want you to stop relying on the opportunities created by others (and living off the adrenaline of that urgent opportunity) and start creating opportunities of your own. You can develop a mindset that's going to make this easier and easier to accomplish. If you know your market and the benefit your customers receive from your art, you can create opportunities to serve them. You can create opportunities to share your work, rather than waiting to seize opportunities. I would like this to be your new mantra,

I don't wait for opportunities, I create opportunities.

Notice that I didn't say create 'product.' You do a fine job creating product. I know you can create product. I said, "create the opportunities to create the product."

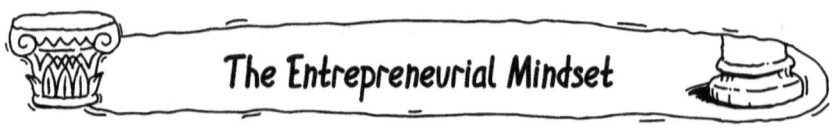

The Entrepreneurial Mindset

There are four things that make up the entrepreneurial mindset. You possess them because you are an artist.

Number 1. You must leverage every opportunity.

Every opportunity that you have for creating, performing, displaying, or speaking about your art must be leveraged to create the next opportunity, to gather more fans, and even to repeat the same opportunity again in a different location at a different venue for a different audience. I want you to stop the pattern of reach into the universe, create it, then dump it. And then go create something else that's new, and then dump that. And then go create something else that's new and dump that. I want you to get out of that pattern, and I want you to start leveraging every opportunity.

Number 1. You can repackage and repurpose.

You create a lot of IP (intellectual property) every time you create something. If you can capture the list of ingredients of the creation, record the steps of the process, or list the parts of the process, or describe them, or explain them, or show them, or demonstrate them, you have just created more products that you can share with the world. People pay to learn to do something or to learn how to do something better or to see how someone else does something.

Number 1. Be consistent and stay the course.

Most small businesses take between three and five years to turn a profit. You usually don't see a profit in a small business for the first three years. By the third year of your business you want to have more money than it takes to create the art and run the business. It's important to be consistent and stay the course because, as artists, we have the 'shiny object syndrome.' We like to create and we're desperately looking for the one thing that's going to work, always creating new things. We move around too fast, we aren't consistent. What I am asking you to do is to think about your arts practice as your arts business. Be consistent and stay the course. When you're running a business that has grown out of your arts practice, the measure of success is not only about profit, it's about viability. And the recipe for the viability of your arts business only has two ingredients: Is there a market for it? And do you still want to do it?

Number 4. Have a voracious curiosity.

Entrepreneurs are voraciously curious. We are lifelong learners. We show up to every experience in life and say, "What can I learn?"

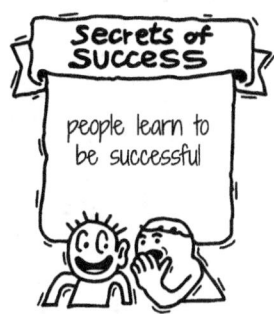

When you read the biographies of successful people, you quickly discover that they learned to be successful. Sure, they have an entrepreneurial mindset, and they are voracious learners, but they learned to be successful. They tried, they failed, they learned, they tried again, and they learned some more. I love this quote from Eric Hoffer:

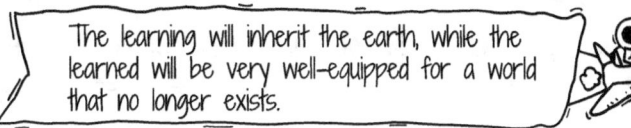

The learning will inherit the earth, while the learned will be very well-equipped for a world that no longer exists.

You were born as an artist entrepreneur, and you can leverage that ability and learn to be a small business entrepreneur. It's up to you to do three things:

- **Have an incredible curiosity about your success.**

- **Have a burning desire to commit yourself to building your arts business.**

- **Be willing to invest your time and money to learn everything you need to know to make your business succeed.**

We can help you get the skills you need. There are at least 92 discrete skills required to run a successful small arts business. It's up to you to learn them.

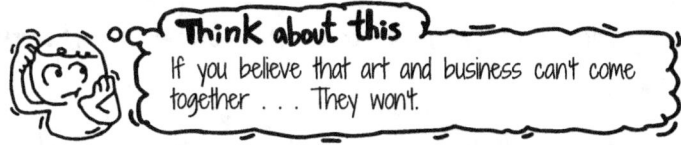

Think about this
If you believe that art and business can't come together . . . They won't.

Your beliefs author your destiny. That's why you need to adjust your mindset.

I'm here to tell you that you can learn to develop a range of revenue streams that all flow from your talent and creativity. I'm here to tell you that you can learn to develop so much confidence and self-esteem that you will be paid well for your time and your art.

I'm here to tell you that you can learn to develop a database of fans, customers, and followers who will eagerly wait for your next creation and will market you.

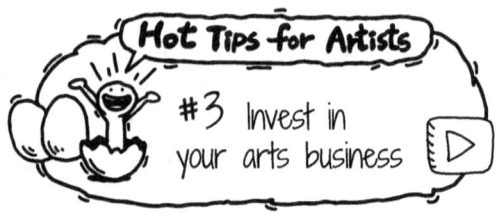

Habits and Behaviours of Success

Success leaves a trail. Lots of coaches and authors have studied successful people in the arts, in politics, and in business, and there are common habits and behaviours that you can observe, learn, and adopt. The top seven habits of successful artists are as follows:

1. exude joy (people want to be around happy people)

2. compliment others (generosity feels better than bitterness)

3. accept responsibility for your failures (it puts you in control)

4. keep a journal (the more you learn about you the better)

5. set goals and develop plans (we are good at hitting goals)

6. operate from a transformational perspective (everything and everyone can change)

7. learn continuously (you and your art are getting better and better)

You don't have to adopt all seven of these practices today, but pick one for this week, and then pick another one for the next week, and focus on that. See if you can learn those habits of success.

Exercise

ARE YOU CAPABLE OF BEING SUCCESFUL?

Y   N

+ Do you have a range of revenue streams that all come from your talent and your creativity? ☐ ☐

+ Do you have the confidence and self-esteem to be paid well for your time and your art? ☐ ☐

+ Do you have a database of fans, customers, and followers who are eagerly awaiting your next creation? ☐ ☐

Pause and take this little diagnostic. These are three things that you need as an artist entrepreneur. Knowing that you don't have any one of these starts you on your journey to get it.

Story of Success
Andrew Follows

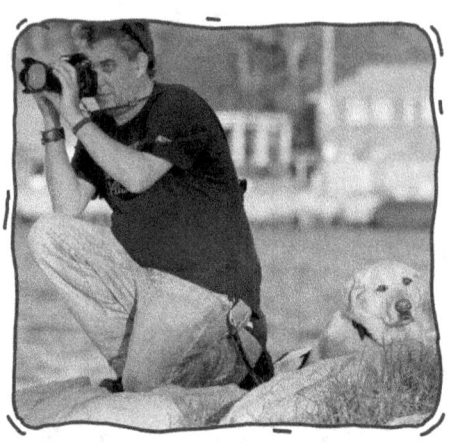

I'd like you to meet an incredible photographer. His name is Andrew Follows. When Andrew first came into the Auspicious Arts Incubator, he was dealing with some of the issues that I'm sure you are experiencing, such as,

✓ *"I don't think I can make a living from my art."*

✓ *"I don't have control of my time."*

✓ *"I'm not charging enough for my products. I don't know what to charge."*

✓ *"I don't have enough fans or customers."*

When we first met Andrew, he did the occasional exhibition and was making hardly any money at all from his photography. But Andrew did have two things:

1. **a burning desire to commit to building his photography business;**

2. **a willingness to invest his time and money to learn everything there was to learn to make his business succeed.**

Oh, I forgot to mention that Andrew is blind.

Andrew worked with us for six months. A year after he worked with us, he dropped by the incubator to hand me a flyer for his next exhibition. It was at a very well-established commercial gallery. I hadn't seen Andrew for several months because he'd been in Europe exhibiting and in Scotland teaching workshops at an international exhibition.

In addition to selling his photographs, creating and curating exhibitions, he is now being paid well to design and conduct workshops to inspire and help other blind photographers. He also has a couple of other moneymaking irons in the fire, but I think you get the picture.

The bottom line is that Andrew knew that there were skills he needed as a business owner that were different from being a talented photographer. As he learned and developed those skills, he also developed a range of revenue streams that all came from his photography. He developed so much confidence and self-esteem that he tripled the price for his time and his artwork. Andrew also developed a database of fans, customers, and followers. He has such strong relationships with his customers now that they eagerly buy his work online and pack the house at every gallery opening.

I hope that this chapter has helped you claim your identity as the Entrepreneurial Artist you have always been. You have what it takes. Every time you create art and share it with others, you're an entrepreneur. All I'm asking you to do is to understand that same process of creation and use those abilities to develop your arts business.

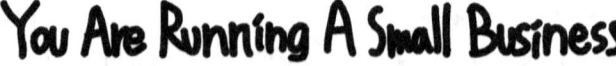

You Are Running A Small Business

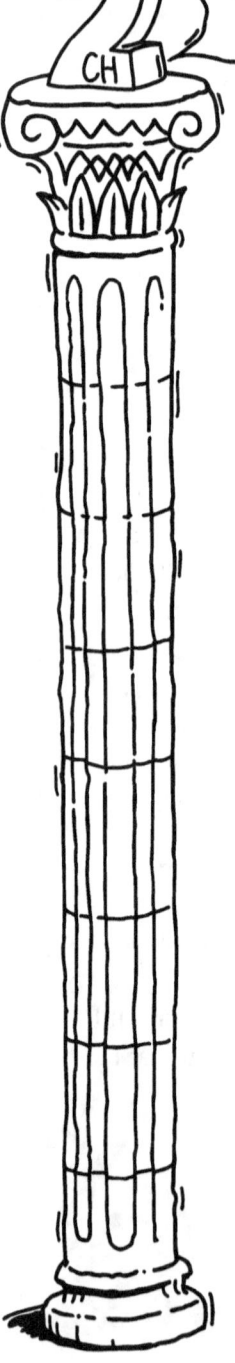

You, like most of us, didn't set out to run a business. You have talent and a desire to create. You have powerful visions, and you're good at manifesting those visions, so you do that. You follow the muse. You create art. You create art products. You create art services. The reality is that when you create services and products, you're running a small business. The evidence that you are in business is that you have customers who buy your products and services, and maybe you have students who want to sign up to your workshops and are paying money to be enrolled. Once you have customers and a product or a service, you're running a small business. The problem is that no one ever explained to you that this is what will eventually happen to us as artists. At least nobody did to me. They encouraged me to develop my talent, but no one explained that one day my talent and my abilities could be the foundation of creating a small business. That's why I'm focusing on helping you to build this pillar of Vision & Mindset. Because at some point, you must switch to the mindset of being an artist in business. And that moment is NOW.

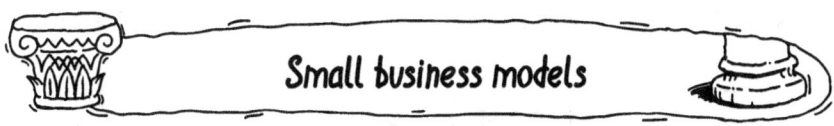

Small business models

As an artist in business, it's important to look at how small businesses other than arts businesses get created. I'd like you to look at this diagram.

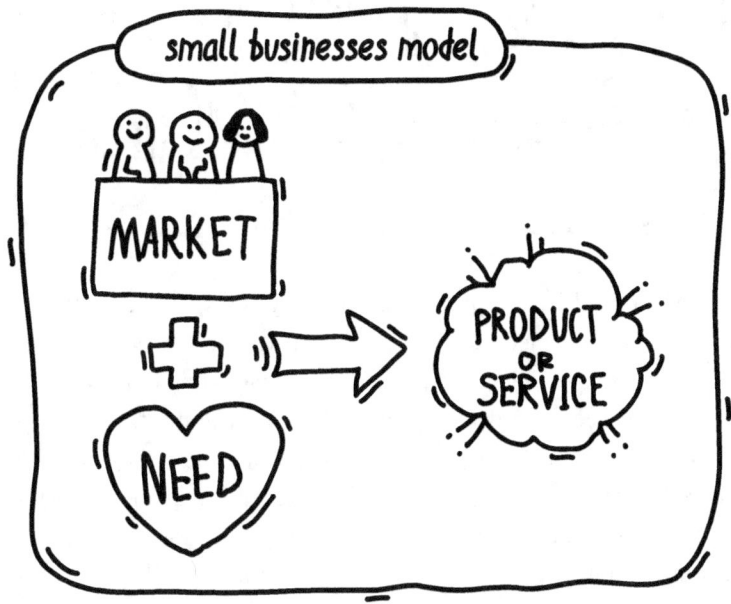

Most small businesses are planned. An entrepreneur finds a need and a market with that need, and then they go and create a product or a service to meet that specific need of that specific market.

For example, someone realised that there was a need for good coffee where they live. They then figured out who needed that good coffee. When they talked to those people, they discovered that they did in fact need good coffee. They learned what 'good' meant to them. They also learned that this particular market needed good fast coffee in the morning and a comfortable place to gather for coffee meetings in the afternoon. So, they created a coffee service and café that would provide these two services and meet the needs of that market.

Unlike in this example, most artists create the product or the service first.

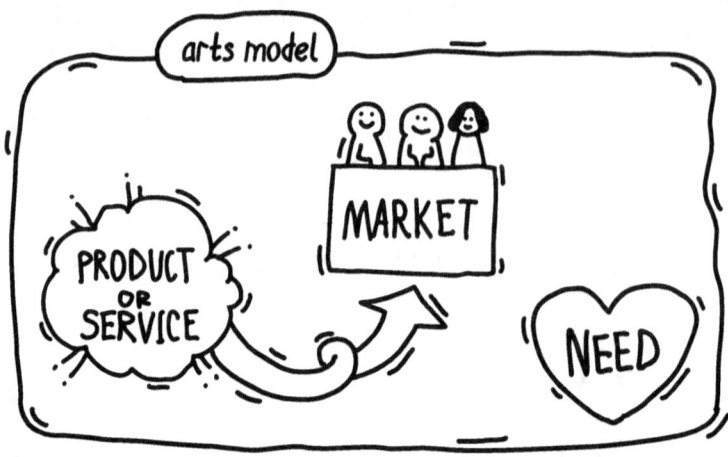

We create beautiful art. We produce an amazing show. We perform a brilliant concert. We write a piece of music. We create the product or the service first, without a market and without a clear understanding of how our product or our service meets the needs of our potential customers. And that's OK. As artists, we don't only create work that people know they want. Part of our success lies in creating products and services that they haven't even imagined. I just want you to understand that for any small business to be successful, including a small arts business, you need to be conscious of all three ingredients required for a business.

You as the CEO of your business, you as the entrepreneur, need to know who the market is for your product or service, and what needs your products or service meets for that market. Once you know that, you can find other markets with those same needs, and if you want to, you can possibly develop more products or services to meet those same needs again. It's fine that you create the product or the service first, but your business is not going to become successful unless you figure out who the market is and how your product or service meets the needs of that market. To succeed as a business, you need to be aware of the connection of all three: the market, the need, and the product or the service. So, you see, as a small business, we're not so unique. We just build our business model in the reverse order.

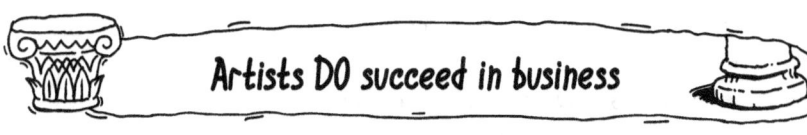

Another point that I would like to make is that in my experience,

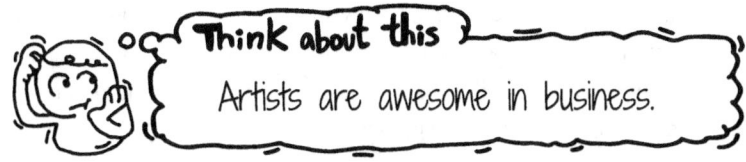

Reflect on this. You deliver your product or service on time and on budget 99% of the time. There are businesses, corporations, and government organisations that never achieve that rate of successful delivery. If they knew about our track record of on-time, on-budget delivery, they would be very envious. For most businesses and organisations, it would be a dream to deliver on time and on budget, even 60% of the time. But you know that you deliver on time. You deliver on budget. You probably even deliver under budget, and you do it consistently. An advertised opening night will happen on the set day. The product will be delivered. The show must go on. The exhibition will open. If that is the day we have declared, it's going to happen on that day, because we make it happen. We guarantee it, and we do it over and over, so we must be good at it.

Another reason that I know artists are awesome in business is that we manage complex projects with a variety of stakeholders. The vision that we're manifesting is often very complex and contains different kinds of ingredients. Different kinds of arts disciplines mixing. Different talents all coming together. We create complex things that have never been seen before. Chemical processes that have never existed before. Mixed media, concepts that have never been tried before. We also have a variety of partners. We negotiate with suppliers. We invite and manage collaborators. Managing all of that is an incredible business skill.

Another reason that artists are awesome at business is that we invent systems and exceed expectations. Quite often, we're creating something that's never been done before. So we have to invent new systems and procedures. We figure out how this thing will happen, how it gets packed up and broken down and reassembled. What's going to hold it together? What are the steps? We invent entire business systems to make an art project, a performance, a concert, or an exhibition happen. Through all of this, we pursue excellence. We constantly exceed expectations. I bet you, when you think about it, people often say to you, "Wow. That's so much more exciting than I imagined. Wow, I never thought it would be like that." And for a business owner to constantly exceed expectations is quite an achievement.

Another reason that we artists are awesome in business is that we conquer obstacles. Because we're driven by vision and passion, we don't accept obstacles but conquer them. We say, "Right, that didn't work, let's find another way. Oh, that looks like crap. Let's find another way. Oh, that doesn't fit. Let's figure something else out." We are constantly course correcting and constantly conquering obstacles. We are very rarely defeated. If there are obstacles in the way, we go over them, we go around them, oftentimes we even incorporate them into our work. This nimble ability we have to manage obstacles is what businesses pay lots of money to acquire. That's another revenue stream to explore.

Another reason that we artists are awesome at business is that we manifest resources. Quite often when we're doing a show, opening an exhibition, or creating a concert, the resources required to make it happen don't yet exist. We find the talent. We find the money. We find the space. We find the partners. Once we know what we need, we are very adept at acquiring those resources and making it happen. This is another skill that most business people envy.

I know that artists are awesome at business. We just never stop long enough to realise how awesome we are. We deploy business skills in the creation of our art—we just don't realise it.

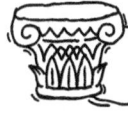 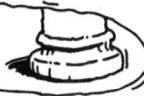

You are in the EMOTION business

Another thing we don't realise is that we are in the emotion business. Artists are often surprised when I say this. You create emotional experiences for others using the medium of your art. Your art is the instrument for generating an emotion in the participant, the observer, the listener, or the viewer. Your customers have an emotional experience—that's the true gift of your art. Your art is often a catalyst for discussion, for thought, for feeling. We are powerful emotion generators. Emotion is the benefit that we provide and the need that we meet for our markets. It's important for you to realise this so that you can learn to talk about this as your true business.

Sara Catena is an artist that we worked with. After completing the course, she learned that she's a happiness catalyst. When she talks to her fans, her followers, and her customers and asks them what they feel when they look at her work, they say, "Your work makes me happy." Well, now that she knows that she's in the business of generating happiness, it's easier for her to find the market that has the need for her art. She is also able to create other products and services that create happiness.

Imagination and intuition are two great attributes. Most small business owners do not have your powerful imagination nor the intuition and the easy ability to converse with their intuition.

I want you to open a dialogue with your intuition. If you've never had a conversation with your intuition in this way, give it a try. As the CEO of your arts business, you need to draw on your inner wisdom.

One of the best ways to converse with your intuition is to ask it a question and then just record the response on paper using the stream of consciousness technique.

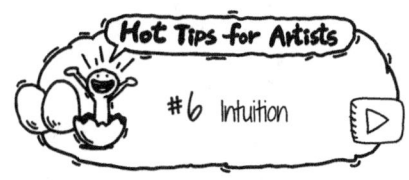

Hot Tips for Artists

#6 Intuition

Pause and do this exercise now.

Set a timer for four minutes.

Ask your intuition the question in the box below and then just let your hand write whatever comes up. Don't think. Don't edit as you write, just write. It's ok to write in this book.

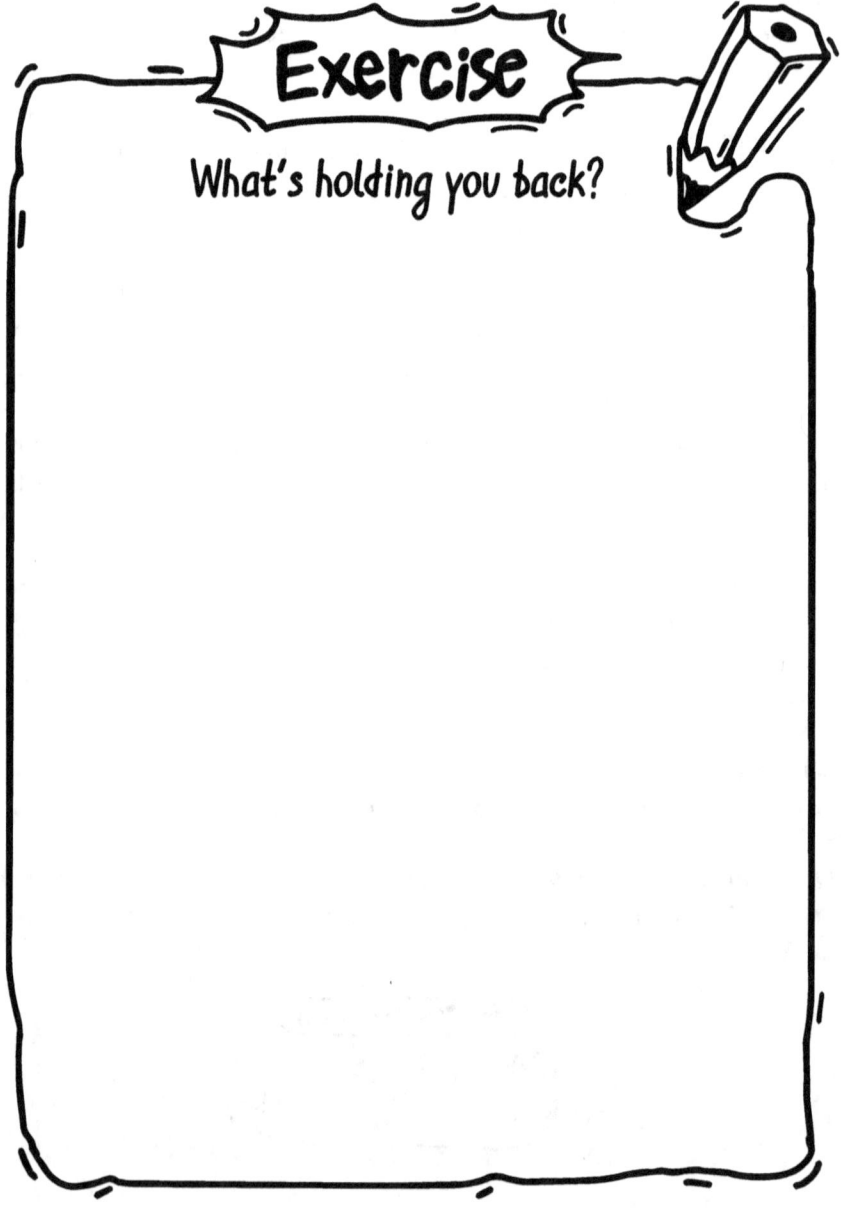

Exercise

What's holding you back?

The wisdom that your intuition shared with you is part of the story that you use to explain why you're where you are. I understand that what you wrote might be true, but that story may not be helping you. If you believe that what's holding you back are things that can't be changed, remember, 80% of success is psychological, so if that's what you believe, it's true.

Perhaps it was true yesterday but could start to change today and be different by tomorrow. Look at what you wrote and think about what you can do to change it. You are running a small business. It's your job to see what's holding you back and change it. Learn the skills you need, so that whatever is holding you back today becomes part of a new story about what used to be holding you back and is no longer preventing you from being successful. Every small business owner learns lessons, course corrects, makes changes, and grows. The same will happen to you when you're running your small arts business.

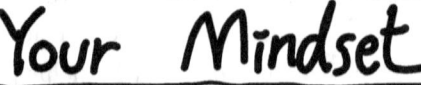

Your Mindset

Because of your ability to manifest your visions, this is the most important chapter in this first section on Vision & Mindset. Your imagination, your emotions, and your passion work together to create amazing art. You've done it before, and you will do it again, so you believe that you can create amazing art. The secret to being successful in your arts business is to believe that you can create a successful arts business. It is the same mindset you have when you create successful art. The key is to learn how your mind works and from what mindset you are operating.

I'm saying it again just so you take it to heart. It's true!

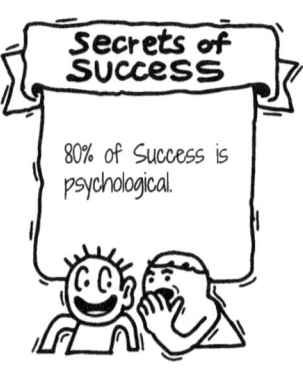

I mentioned in the section on how to use this book that my journey took some interesting detours as I developed the skills and the knowledge to help artists learn to be better at business. When I started the Auspicious Arts Incubator, I realised that there were some psychological obstacles that prevented many artists from being successful in business. My team and I realised that they held beliefs that were limiting their success. Either they didn't believe in themselves, or they didn't believe in their art. They believed that they weren't good at business, and that they were bad with money. They believed that money and business ruined the art. Fundamentally, they didn't believe in themselves as successful artists in business.

I realised that there were some things that we needed to learn if we were going to help artists correct those beliefs and build confidence. We set out on a journey to find the psychological tools that worked best to help clarify and correct faulty beliefs. We needed to find the tools that would help develop the mindset of an artist in business. This journey took four years, but we found out how the artist's mind works, how to defeat limiting beliefs, how to build confidence, and how to acquire new habits. Along the way, we created an entire course to conquer limiting beliefs, develop confidence, and operate at peak performance. And that course is called **The Artist's Mojo.**

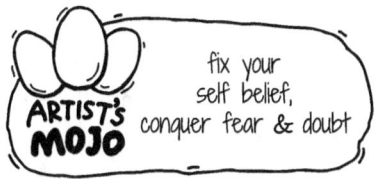

You can go to our website to find out more. Make the journey to change your beliefs and develop the mindset of a successful artist in business. If 80% of success is psychological, then your mind is the key to your success, isn't it?

The first skill that you must develop is the mindset of an artist who is successful in business. It's important to look at the beliefs you have around business, around artists in business, and around yourself in business. It's your beliefs, that create your thoughts, your emotions, and your actions that deliver your results.

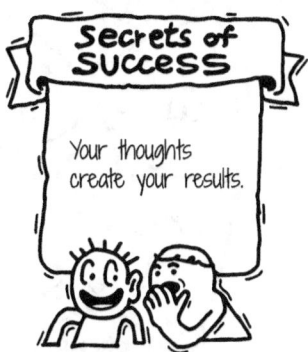

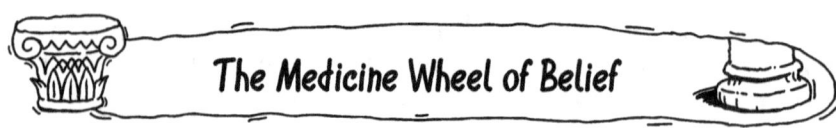

The Medicine Wheel of Belief

I'd like to introduce you to the concept of the medicine wheel. Earlier, I explained to you that one of the detours in my life was becoming apprentice to a medicine woman. I learned a lot sitting at the feet of indigenous elders and medicine men and women. Most of this wisdom was shared using a medicine wheel. Whenever there was something I needed to understand, my teacher would pick up a stick and draw a circle on the earth as the foundation of the lesson.

A medicine wheel describes a cycle. It explains how things move around the circle and helps us understand relationships. I'd like to introduce you to the medicine wheel of belief.

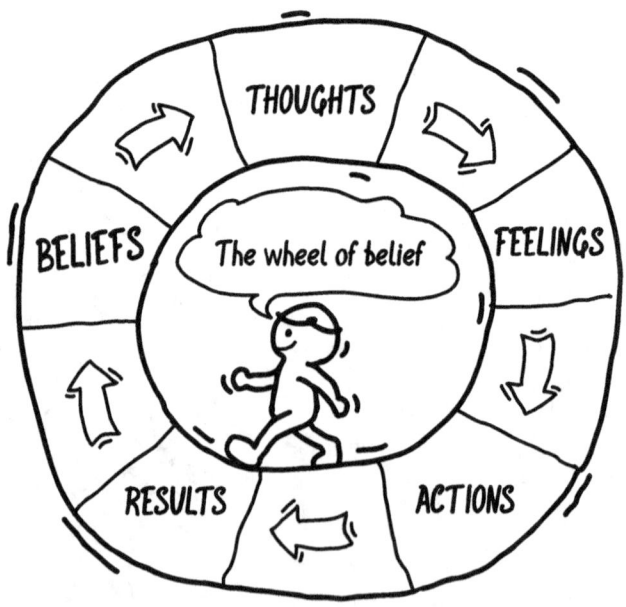

This wheel shows us that

Your beliefs create thoughts,

and those thoughts create feelings,

and those feelings create actions,

and those actions create results.

Your results are the evidence you need to support a belief, which will generate more thoughts, and those thoughts (the things that you're saying out loud and inside your mind) create an emotion (a state of being). And because of those thoughts and emotions, you take action, or you don't take action. Your inaction or your action creates the results that you have in your life. Do you see how it works?

The awesome thing about this medicine wheel of beliefs is that it also offers you the remedy to fix things that aren't working for you. If something isn't good in your life as an artist in business, see where that is on the wheel.

For example, let's say you're in a real funk. You're not feeling good, you're not feeling motivated. Well, look at this medicine wheel and say, "Hmm, the discomfort is in my feelings." The remedy for it is to go back one stage and ask, "What are the thoughts that I'm having? Those thoughts created this feeling, so, what was I thinking that's making me have this unpleasant feeling?" The remedy for the feelings is to change your thoughts. You can go back one more stage and say, "Well, why am I thinking these thoughts?" And you're going to find some belief at the core of all of this. The ultimate remedy for these feelings is to find a belief that's better. Some of your beliefs have created these thoughts. Those thoughts then created the unpleasant feelings you are experiencing now. Your ultimate job is to find a belief that will create positive thoughts, which will then generate positive feelings and start the wheel moving in a positive direction. The new feelings inspire positive actions that yield the results you desire.

Similarly, let's say that you don't have the results you want. Let's say you don't have the money you want. Well, back up one stage. What actions are you taking that are giving you this result? "I'm not doing the marketing. I'm not making those calls. I'm not following up with those opportunities." Back up a stage. Why aren't you doing any of this? "Well, because I don't feel confident." Why don't you feel confident? "Because I say to myself, 'I don't know what I'm doing. I don't know how to succeed.'" And why are you thinking those thoughts? "Well, because I believe I'm a fraud." Ah. Well, what if we change that belief to something more helpful, such as, "When I first started out, I didn't know what I was doing, but after seven years, I'm confident that my art is good." And off you go to get better results.

This is a very powerful tool. Draw this medicine wheel of beliefs and post it on your wall. Start using this tool. It will educate you about your mindset and how your beliefs are authoring your business results.

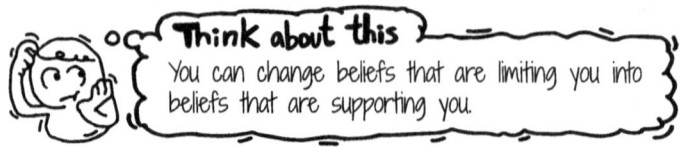

Think about this
You can change beliefs that are limiting you into beliefs that are supporting you.

We CAN change beliefs. I've seen it. I've experienced it. You can stop using old beliefs. You can adopt new beliefs. Note: you can't delete an old belief. It is hardwired into your subconscious for life. What you can do is to stop using it. You can create new neural pathways that move around that belief. Eventually it becomes part of the story of how you used to be. You can install a new positive belief in your subconscious that's going to get you the results you want and generate the thoughts you want, which will generate the feelings you want, which will in turn produce the actions, which will finally get you the results you need.

You can get help with changing beliefs. It's a thing.

We have specially trained coaches who have ways of helping artists change their beliefs and install positive ones. Two of the strongest belief-changing techniques for artists are NLP—Neuro-linguistic Programming—and Psych-K. These two practices are absolutely brilliant for developing positive beliefs and developing your mindset as a successful artist in business.

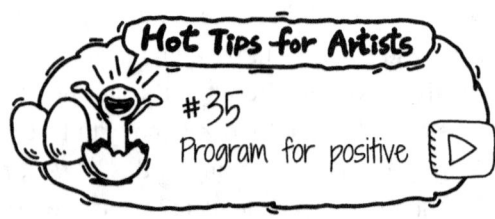

Hot Tips for Artists
#35
Program for positive ▷

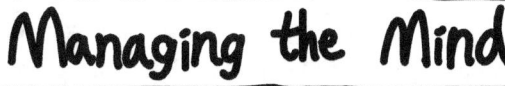

Managing the Mind

As we move through this section on Vision & Mindset, it's also important for you to learn to get better at managing your mind and managing your emotions. The subject of how to manage emotions is covered in the final section of the book. In this chapter, we're going to look at some of the ways to manage the mind. As you learned in the last chapter, the thoughts that we have are the things that will help propel your business to success or hold you back. It's crucial that you learn to manage your mind. This is way beyond simply understanding psychology.

There are eleven key aspects to what's commonly referred to as your brain or your mind. The brain and the mind are terms for complex systems and physical structures.

Neuroscience tells us that we have three brains.

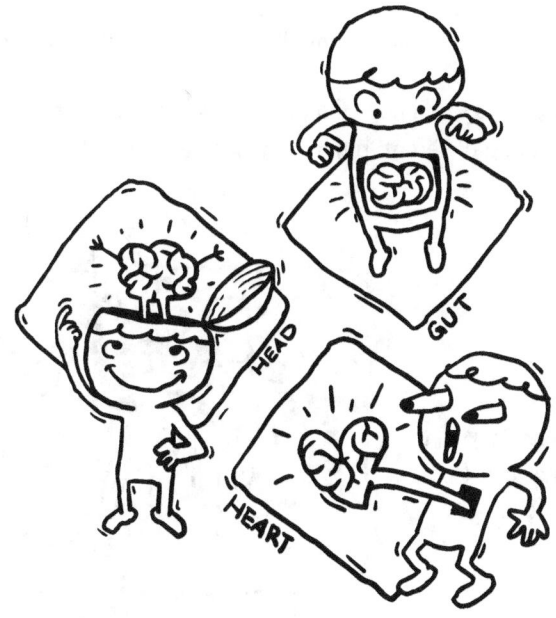

There's a brain that's in your head, there's a brain that's in your heart, and there's a brain that's in your gut. All three are involved in decision-making. You know about the one in your head. Thoughts, opinions, and logic make decisions in your head, your reasoning brain. You also experience feelings and desires that seem to make decisions for you, that come from the brain that's in your heart. Actually, a ganglion of nerves is located around the heart, and that's where you have the feelings of love and desire. You've heard people say, "My heart's just not in it." There's another ganglion of nerves centred in your gut. You've experienced that brain when you say, "Oh, I just have a gut feeling about it." That's your gut brain trying to tell you that this is safe or not safe for you.

If you find this intriguing, I encourage you to pause and go look up 'the three brains.' When you need to make a decision for your arts business, it's important for you to consult all three.

"OK, head brain, what do you say about this opportunity?"

"OK, heart brain, what do you feel about this opportunity?"

"OK, gut brain, what do you know about this opportunity?"

Listen to the wisdom from all three brains before you come to a decision.

Evolutionary science also teaches us that we have three brains, but it means something different in that context: the Triune Brain.

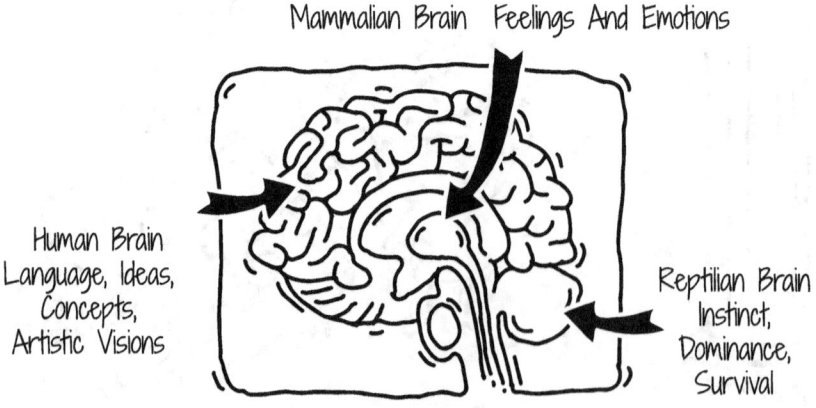

Mammalian Brain — Feelings And Emotions

Human Brain — Language, Ideas, Concepts, Artistic Visions

Reptilian Brain — Instinct, Dominance, Survival

Evolutionary scientists talk about the brainstem or the reptilian brain, the midbrain or the mammalian brain, and the neocortex or the primate brain. When you understand how these three brains work, you'll be more successful at pitching, networking, and enlisting others.

Here's an example. When you meet someone new, the first thing that happens is their old reptilian brainstem is activated. The oldest part of their brain fires up first and sizes you up to decide if you are safe or unsafe. That is the only thing that matters to this part of the brain. The person you are meeting is not actually listening to anything you say, because the rest of the brain is waiting for the brainstem to make the call about whether you are safe or unsafe. If you leap too quickly into a networking conversation and start talking immediately about your art, no one's going to hear you. They're not paying attention. They're just trying to figure out whether you are safe or unsafe. Spend that first 30 seconds being open, exposing yourself, arms wide, chest high, eyes focused. Allow the person's reptilian brain to size you up as safe. Give them non-verbal signals that say, "I'm safe."

If you succeed at this, the reptilian brain passes you forward to the person's midbrain. Their mammalian midbrain is where you get the emotional memory scan. It's up to the midbrain to decide whether to give you more attention or not. When their reptilian brain says, "OK, you're safe," the midbrain asks, "Hmm, do I want any of what you have?" This is the point in a networking conversation where you want to be a good listener, where you want to be empathetic, where you want to have good rapport, because you want your audience's midbrain to say, "Oh yes, I like this person. I want more of this person. This is interesting." When the midbrain is intrigued and wants more, it gives you the green light and passes you on to the neocortex. That's where conscious thoughts and all data is collected. In this networking example, the brainstem says, "OK, you're safe." The midbrain says, "OK, I want more of you," so the human brain says, "So what's your name? How do I find you? Tell me more about this project." It's good to know about these three brains and to understand that the person you're meeting for the first time has three brains that are being activated one after another so that you can structure your interaction to be a positive one.

Physical science explains that there are two halves to our brain.

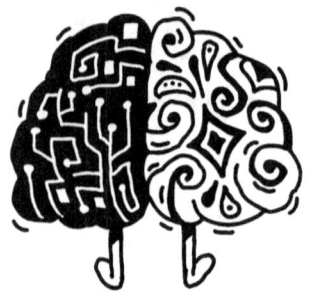

The left hemisphere is for logic and sequences, and the right hemisphere for spatial relationships, emotional memory, and creativity. As artists, most of us have very well-developed right brains. As an artist in business you need to exercise and strengthen the left hemisphere as well. There are exercises called Brain Gyms, specific exercises that get the neurons on both sides of the brain to fire so that you can function from a well-balanced brain. It is useful to know about the two hemispheres of your brain. When you've been creative for a long stretch of time, it's very hard to switch gears and sit down and write some proposals or send out some invoices. And similarly, if you've been spending time exercising the left hemisphere doing invoices, making calls, building schedules, or writing down plans, it's often difficult for you to be creative.

Balancing your brain is a thing. I encourage you to google it. Look for brain gym exercises. You'll find a series of exercises quite often in video format that use your eyes, arms, and legs to activate both the right and left hemispheres of your brain and bring you into balance.

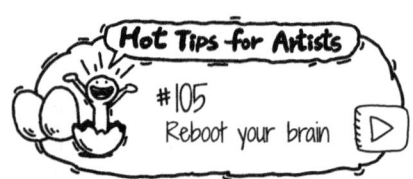

Here's a concrete example of how powerful you can become if you understand the functionality of these two hemispheres of your brain. Remember, the left hemisphere is responsible for critical thinking, and the right hemisphere is for emotion and memory. Let's say that you're trying to gather reactions from your exhibition, or a presentation, or a show. To get comments that you can use for marketing purposes, you want people to respond from the right hemisphere, from their emotional memory. Ask them questions like, "How did this make you feel?"

You never want to ask them a question that takes them over to the left hemisphere like, "What was your favourite?" or "What was the best?". Such questions force the person to move from the emotional side of their brain over to the analytical side. If you do that, the response they give you won't be passionate and emotional. It is not going to make good marketing copy. It'll be analytical.

What you want are 'juicy' emotional comments. So always keep the conversation on the right side of their brain, in the place of memory and emotion, and ask them, Ask questions like, "What's something you remember from this show? How did it make you feel?"

We went down the marketing rabbit hole there only to help you see the value in learning how your mind/brain works.

OK, that's eight of the eleven key aspects of the brain important for you to know. There are still three more. Psychology teaches us that there are three minds that utilise all parts of the brain.

These three minds are the conscious mind, the subconscious mind, and the superconscious mind. To explain why this matters for an artist in business, I'd like to concentrate on just two of the three, the subconscious and the conscious. It is important for you to understand how these two minds play out in our lives. Once we understand what they do and how they work, we can make better use of them

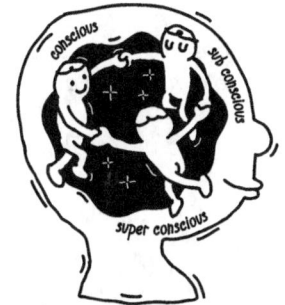

The conscious mind. The conscious mind is volitional. That means that it sets goals, judges results, and thinks abstractly. The conscious mind is also time-bound. It tracks the past and the future. The greatest misuse of the conscious mind is to worry about the future and to regret the past. The only reason that your conscious mind spins around with worry and regret is because it can. Not that it wants to, it's just that it can. It's good at it. It understands what happened in the past and what could happen in the future. Your conscious mind has limited processing capacity. It's where your short-term memory lives. This limited processing capacity means that you can only track one to three events at a time. The idea that we can multitask isn't really true. Your ability to multitask is dependent on your skill at effectively and rapidly shifting your conscious mind's attention between tasks, but only about one to three of them at a time. The other thing about this limited processing capacity is that the conscious mind can only track about forty bits of information per second.

Your subconscious mind is way more powerful than the conscious mind. While the conscious mind was volitional, the subconscious mind is habitual. It learns how you do things and just repeats it. It monitors all the operations of the body: the motor functions, the heart, the lungs, the breathing, the digestion. It just runs the program and executes the functions. It thinks literally. It does not think abstractly. It doesn't understand concepts of 'in the future' or 'in the past'. Nor can it do anything with abstract concepts like 'don't'.

> Here's an example. An actor gives this command to their mind, "Don't blow this audition!" Well, the poor subconscious mind can't think abstractly, so it's confused, "You want something. I can feel the emotional charge, but I can't help you, because of this abstract concept 'don't.' I don't understand the concept of 'don't.' Hmm, what are you trying to get me to do for you? The other three words are 'blow this audition.' OK. I can find you images and memories of blowing this audition. Is that what you want? I can pull up lots of those, and I can create those right now and put you in that mental and emotional state. That must be what you want."

While the conscious mind is time-bound, the subconscious mind doesn't 'do' time. It only operates in the present. You've experienced a smell that triggers a memory, and suddenly you are experiencing that memory as if it's happening right now. Your powerful subconscious mind only operates in the present. It doesn't know whether something is true, false, or imagined. It's literal—it's happening right now, in present time.

And while the conscious mind has limited processing capacity, the subconscious mind has expanded processing capacity. It's where your long-term memory is located. It's where your past experiences, your attitudes, your values, and your beliefs are kept. They're all stored in your subconscious. The expanded processing capacity of the subconscious mind allows it to handle thousands of events at the same time. Your heart can be beating, your food getting digested, your lungs breathing while you are dancing and singing and painting. And all of that is happening simultaneously. Thousands of actions, no problem. And while the poor conscious mind could only track about forty bits of information per second, the subconscious mind can track forty million bits of information per second. As you walk down the street, it processes the temperature of the day, the sounds in the distance, at the same time keeping your body upright. There are literally millions and millions of stimuli coming in, and your subconscious mind sorts them and passes the important ones to the conscious mind and deals with all the rest.

I'm taking the time to explain the conscious mind and the subconscious mind so that you understand how to make changes in your beliefs, thoughts, habits and patterns of behaviour. You can manage your mind to effectively change some beliefs that limit you into beliefs that support you, but the work has to happen inside the subconscious mind, not in the conscious mind.

You cannot change your subconscious mind through the conscious mind. In order to work successfully with your subconscious, I recommend that you work with a tested process with a coach who is an expert, someone who can speak 'subconsciounese.' Many people try to influence the subconscious with the conscious mind, but you can't just tell your conscious mind to do it. If you are trying to change a belief, you must acknowledge that it no longer resides in the conscious mind. Beliefs are held in the subconscious mind and operate and drive your behaviour from there. If you want to install a new belief and get it to drive a different behaviour, it can't be installed in the conscious mind by simply willing it to happen. The subconscious mind must accept it. This is why, for so many artists, positive affirmations do not work. If the subconscious mind doesn't accept them, the affirmations are just empty words that you repeat over and over. You can say, "I am a millionaire" over and over every day, but if your core belief is, "I am a poor and struggling artist," your subconscious mind just filters it away: "What are you saying? That phrase doesn't agree with a core belief. Disregard!"

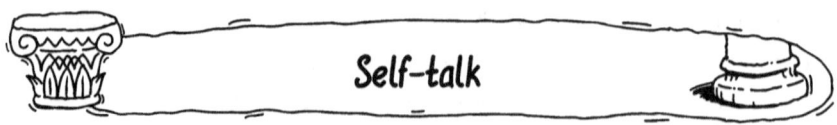

Self-talk

Another critical part of mastering your mind is mastering self-talk. Sometimes the most toxic relationship we have is the one with ourselves. Many of us beat ourselves up. We call ourselves names. We make a mistake and we say, "Oh, you idiot." We obsess about our faults. "I always do this. I always make the same mistake." And we declare ourselves unworthy of love and of happiness. "It's not enough! Work harder. I just have to make this one last thing happen." We flood our mind with doubt, cynicism, and hate, and we continually generate oppressive and disempowering thoughts. When this happens over and over, we become dissociated and discontented. We do this to ourselves.

On the other hand, we can have a relationship with ourselves that is healthier and friendlier. We can nurture ourselves by taking pride in our accomplishments. We can acknowledge our strengths. We can believe that we are worthy of a good life. We can recognise when we do well, when we try our best, when we stand up for what we believe in, when we connect authentically with others. And when we do this, our self-talk focuses on how deserving, capable, trustworthy, and loving we are.

It's time to be your own best friend. Change your self-talk. Your best friend wouldn't talk to you the way you talk to yourself, so change it. Changing what you say to yourself is in your control. Changing the words you use and the thoughts you have is part of managing your mind.

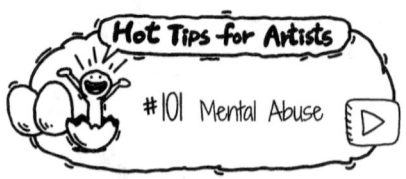

The most important relationship we have, the person we talk to the most, is inside our own mind. As an independent artist, we are solo entrepreneurs. We don't have a boss who's going to congratulate us. We don't have co-workers who are going to rush in to cheer us on. It's entirely up to us.

Story of Success
Lindy Bayley / MABBATT

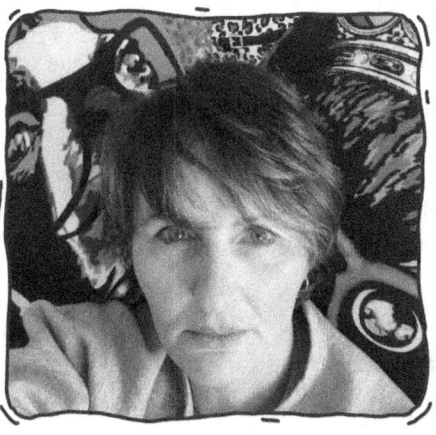

When we first met Lindy Bayley, aka MABBATT, she'd completely lost confidence in herself as an artist and had mental blocks about being an artist. She described her arts practice as erratic. When she felt the urge, she would pick up the art. She'd have a burst of creativity and would then let it drop. For fifteen years after art school, she'd pick it up for a month or so, create something sensational, but do nothing with it. Lindy didn't exhibit at all between the time she left art school until after she finished our Artist's Mojo course.

Reflecting on the artist she is now, Lindy says, "The negative mindset stuff isn't there anymore. It took a process to totally clear it, and it's gone. Right now, it's hard to remember what it was like. The fear that was associated with putting my work out there was blocking me so much that I wasn't putting anything out there. I didn't have a vision of myself as a successful artist. I was blocked in the way I perceived art and myself as an artist. I couldn't say I was an artist. It was like I was claiming to be something I wasn't. I was lying, making myself a target for criticism."

Instead of making art and being the awesome artist she is, Lindy was just letting the rest of her life take over all her time and energy.

But it wasn't the life she wanted to be living.

Finally, Lindy reached out for help. She enrolled in the Artist's Mojo course, to sort out her beliefs, regain her confidence, and put herself out there. Using NLP and Psych-K, the team and I worked through massive issues in a really short period of time. This allowed Lindy to become a successful artist and to embrace her success.

Lindy attributes her fundamental shift to the one-on-one coaching sessions that are part of the Artist's Mojo course. "It never dawned on me that you could get counselling for art and creativity. I looked at the barriers to my creativity. Why wasn't I pursuing things? Why had I lost confidence? What were the risks of my getting back out there? What were the negatives I'd experienced previously that were lodged in my brain? Whenever I'd start on something creative, there were all these negative things that I really didn't know were there, saying things like, 'Oh you really don't want to do that again.'" We helped Lindy clear her negative beliefs, many of which were rooted in her childhood. She had negative perceptions about being an artist that had been in her head for a very long time. The biggest one was being told, "Being an artist isn't a real job." The Mojo course changed all of that. I remember that Lindy phoned me just prior to coming in for her final coaching session to say that we had to be quick, because right after, she had to go to a newspaper interview about her and her art. I'd say she'd gotten her mojo back.

With her restored mojo, Lindy went straight into the Artist's Transformation School. She strengthened her vision and mindset and consolidated the business aspects of her practice with the vision of herself as a successful artist. Like many artists, Lindy never thought of herself as a business person. She learned how to get a handle on making money, covering costs, and measuring money coming in and going out. The ATS has changed the way she works and helped her to diversify her income. She's also using Instagram and other social media effectively to get herself and her art out there.

Lindy has struck a positive balance between her life and her art. She creates every day. She's given up her day job, and in addition to exhibiting her art and jewellery, she sells prints and other items online to international markets in the USA, the UK, Japan, Ireland, France, New Zealand, and Australia. She's also creating digital art on her iPad. She's using her new business and marketing skills for exciting community projects, political knitting (which is gaining momentum), developing gardens at a heritage building, and coordinating a huge visual arts festival in her town for the second year in a row.

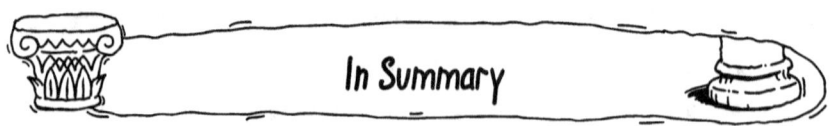

In Summary

I think you can see why working on your Vision & Mindset is important for you as an artist in business. There are things limiting your vision and controlling your mindset. Once you get clear on where you're heading, you see the vision of your arts business, and you've adopted the right mindset, you will achieve it. That's what happens when you create your art, isn't it? Establishing your business may require some new skills, some new thinking, even some new beliefs.

Get your vision clear, and develop a positive mindset. If you don't have a clear, powerful, and compelling vision and are not operating from the mindset of the successful and powerful artist that you are, get to work on that. I'm here to tell you that you can learn this stuff. Invest the time, invest the money, and get your vision and mindset sorted. You'll continue to flounder and stay in your comfort zone of struggle until you do.

Do something in the next 48 hours or you never will.

As a kinaesthetic visual learner, you know that if you don't do something with the stuff you learned in this section, the learning will disappear.

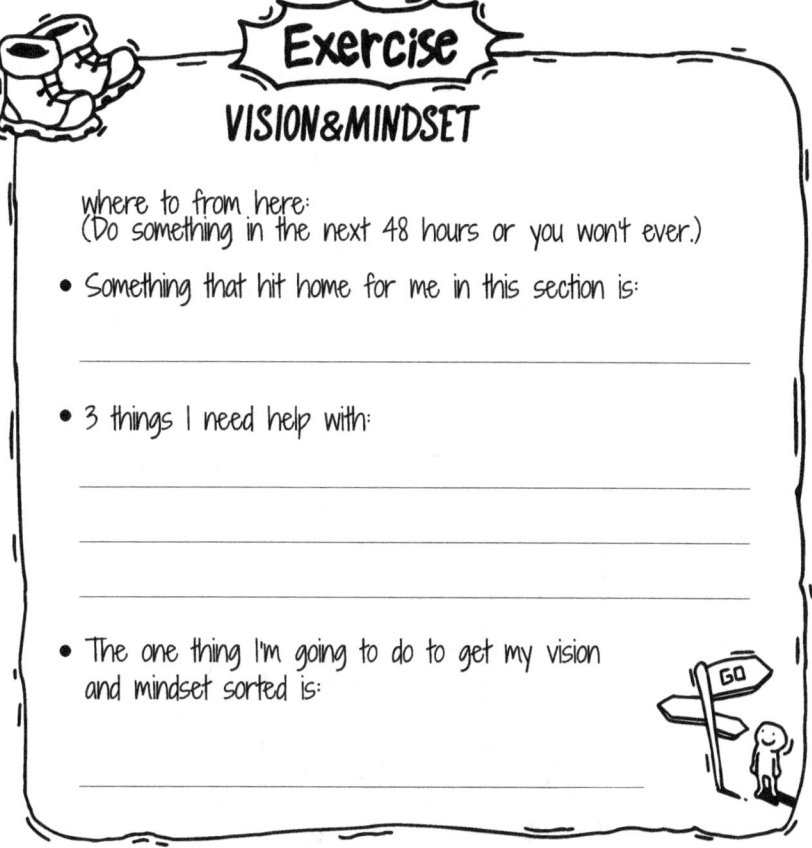

Exercise

VISION&MINDSET

where to from here:
(Do something in the next 48 hours or you won't ever.)

- Something that hit home for me in this section is:

  _____

- 3 things I need help with:

  _____

  _____

  _____

- The one thing I'm going to do to get my vision and mindset sorted is:

  _____

Artists before you have identified six things from this section as being worthy of their focus.

1. I need to develop an entrepreneurial mindset.

2. I'm running a small business.

3. I must get the skills I need.

4. I must change my limiting beliefs.

5. I must walk the wheel of belief.

6. I must monitor my thoughts.

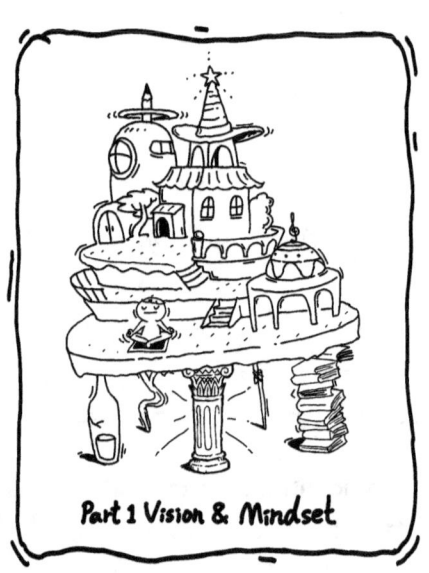

Part 1 Vision & Mindset

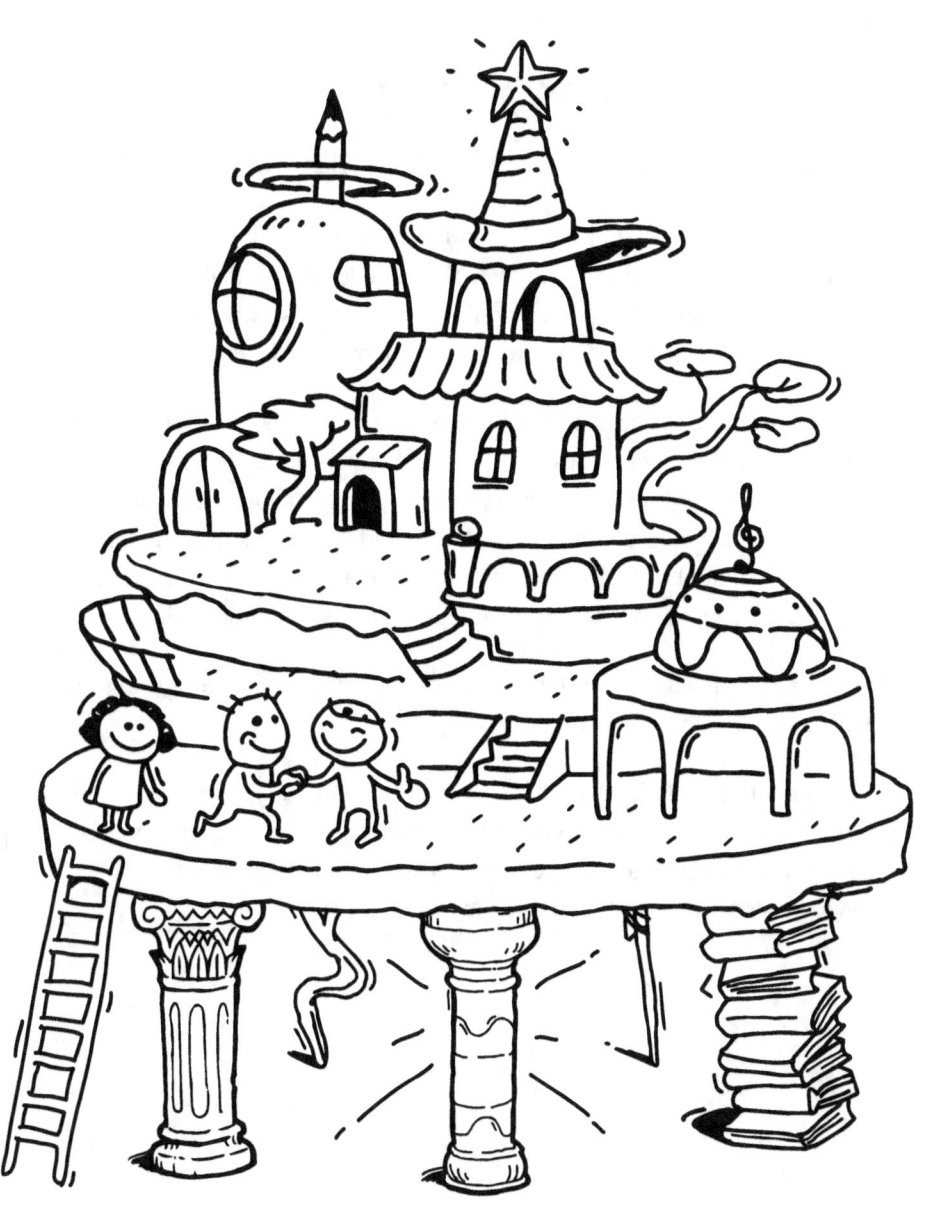

Part 2 Branding & Values

This section looks at two questions:

Why are you doing this?
How do you stay true to what's important to you?

You've got your vision and mindset sorted, you know where you're going, and you believe that you can get there. You need to be sure that other people understand who you are and what you're doing. You also want to make sure that what you're doing is aligned with what's important to you.

As the owner of a successful arts business, you want to be in the position where your market appreciates, respects, and understands you. There needs to be an alignment between what you think you are about and what your customers think you are about. It is also important that there is agreement between your brand and the things that are important to you. Your business is going to grow, so you want to be creating art aligned with your values.

Identifying your values is a fancy way of saying that you're figuring out what's important to you.

This is no longer your hobby. Very soon, you're going to gather people to be on your team. There needs to be an alignment of values between how you see your art in the world and how people who are coming to work with you and support you see your work in the world.

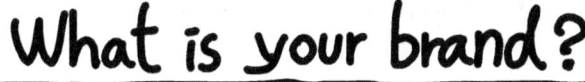

What is your brand?

This chapter asks you to consider two important questions about your art and your arts business. **What are you known for?** And, **Why do people spend their time and their money on you?**

The answer to these questions will determine your brand. When I talk about your brand, I'm are not talking about your logo. Your logo is just part of the visual identity of your brand. Your brand is not painting, acting, singing, dancing, composing or writing—these are merely the things you do. Your brand as an artist is your likeability and enthusiasm. No matter what you think your brand is, when you're active in a marketplace selling your art, the reason that people hire you and buy your art comes down to your likeability and your enthusiasm. It's the reason people want to work with you. Think about it: you want to be involved with people who are likeable and enthusiastic. You don't want to collaborate and work with people who are mean and cranky. If you want to develop a good brand as an independent artist, look at your likeability and your enthusiasm. When you are alone in your studio, you can be whatever you want to be. As an artist in business, you're in the marketplace, you're dealing with customers, you're dealing with partners. Your brand is not your logo. It is not what you do. It is how you do it. Your brand is built on how likeable you are and how enthusiastically you do what you do.

Neil Gaiman suggests that if you want a good brand, you need to be **likeable, be on time, and be good at what you do.**

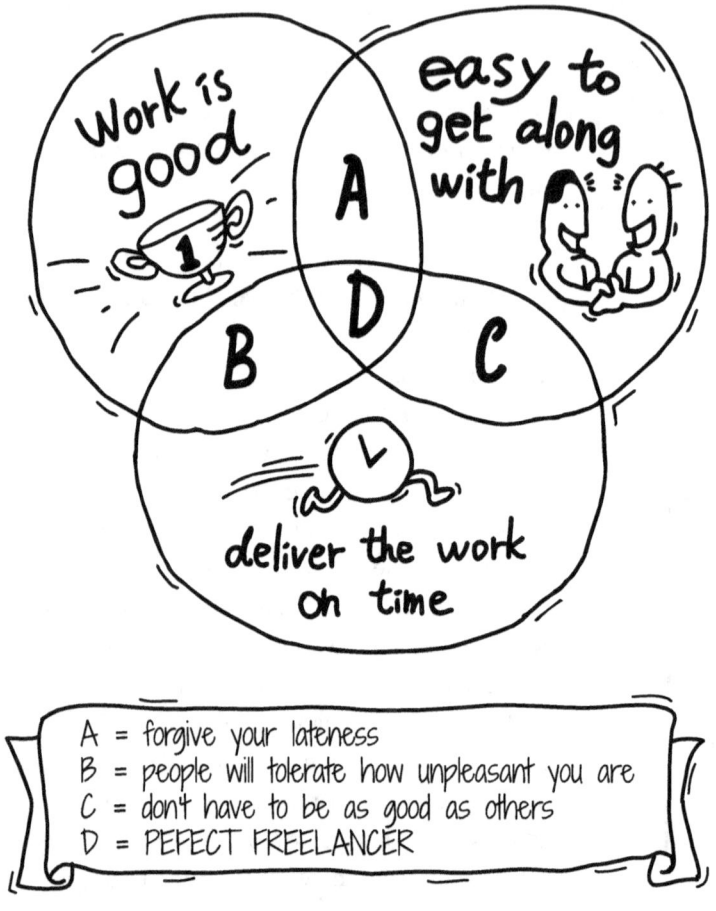

Most people in business can be successful with only two of the three.

If you want to be a successful artist in business, you need to be all three. That way, you can ensure that your brand is solid and that you will have repeat business.

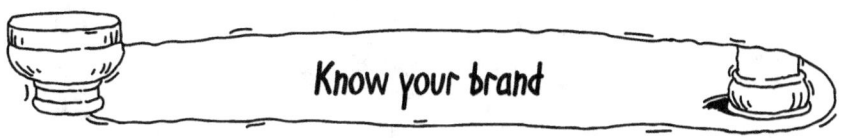

Know your brand

It's essential that you find out what your brand is. As an artist, you already have a brand in play. People have already responded to your likeability and your enthusiasm. People have already had an emotional experience with your art. Start asking your friends, your fans, and your supporters what your brand is. Whatever they say is more valid than what you think. The customer is always right. Start asking them today.

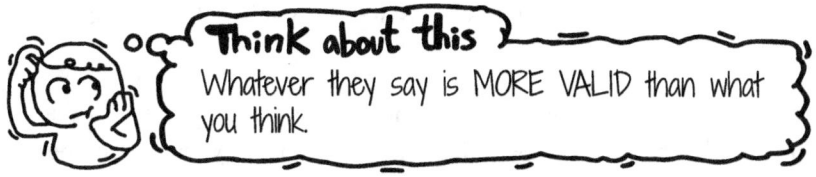

Think about this
Whatever they say is MORE VALID than what you think.

Just ask them, "How do you describe me? How do you describe my art? What do you say I am?" Ask them to give you a score on your likeability and enthusiasm, and see how you fare.

The writer and activist Maya Angelou has a beautiful quote that I love. She says,

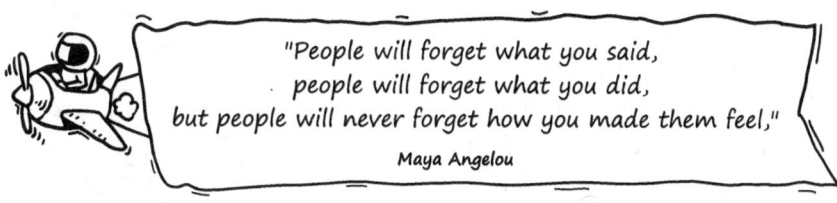

"People will forget what you said,
people will forget what you did,
but people will never forget how you made them feel,"
Maya Angelou

and it's true. That's a huge part of your brand. Here's a little exercise you can do.

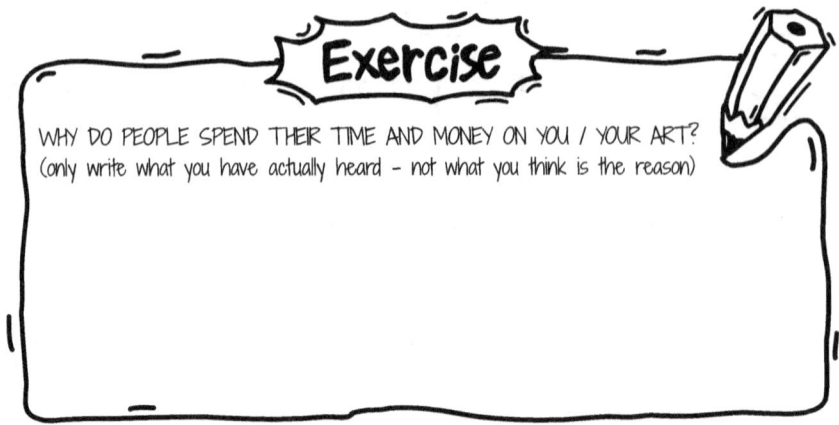

Exercise

WHY DO PEOPLE SPEND THEIR TIME AND MONEY ON YOU / YOUR ART? (only write what you have actually heard - not what you think is the reason)

For this exercise to be useful, only write what you have actually heard. Whatever people say is more valuable to you than what you imagine they might say.

You have a brand in play as an artist in business and you need to share it. Whatever people say, however they describe you and your art, you need to share those exact words. Your brand is about you. It's about sharing who you are, not selling what you have. What you have and what you do are not your brand. Your brand is you. People see you as an amazing, intriguing artist. Selling your art happens by sharing yourself.

You are in the emotion business. Your job, as your brand ambassador, is to ensure that the person receiving your emotional experience realises that it comes from you. It is always your job to remind people, "That cool emotional experience you had with my art was brought to you by me." You are the one who created it—not the venue, and not the producer, nor the

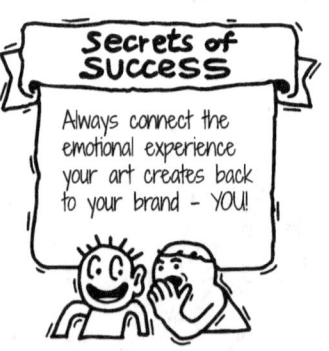

Secrets of Success

Always connect the emotional experience your art creates back to your brand - YOU!

curator. Making this connection is a very important job. It is a job that you must do, because no one else will. You may have to put up signs, you may have to remind people of your name. In whatever way you do it, make sure that people realise that you're the source of the emotional experience they have come for, not the venue. Once they realise that you are the source of their emotion, they'll never forget how you made them feel. They will want to follow your brand, they will want to seek you out.

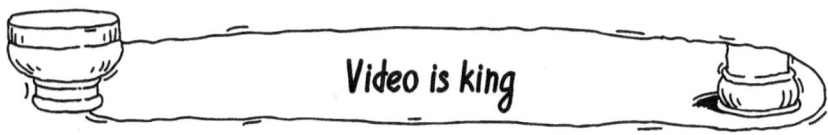

Video is king

The best way to share who you are and to share your likeability and your enthusiasm is through video. Here's a story you might not know. When Google bought YouTube, they did a study to understand how people engage with videos. Along with noting what they watch, Google also wanted to know long they spent watching videos. Here's what they learned. Most people who were investigating a topic would invest 7 seconds in it. That is, they typically watched only the first seven seconds of a video.

A person is willing to find out who you are and get a feel for your brand, but they want to receive that information in the first 7 seconds of your video. After seven seconds, 80% of the viewers leave unless you give them some reason to stay. If there's some reason to stay, they will hang on for up to 18 seconds. At 18 seconds, 80% of those people will leave unless there's a compelling reason to continue, and then they will stay up to 30 seconds. At the 30-second mark, 80% of those people will leave unless there's an even more compelling reason to stay, and they will watch until 90 seconds are up. The only people who are still watching your video after 90 seconds are your absolute target market, your mother, your best friend, and you. We say 'Video is King' because it is by far the best way to share yourself and to give people a sample of your brand. Through a video, they get to see you. They get to see your world. They get to understand who you are, why you do what you do, and can understand some of your values. Based on how likeable and enthusiastic you are in your videos, they will make the decision about whether they want more of you.

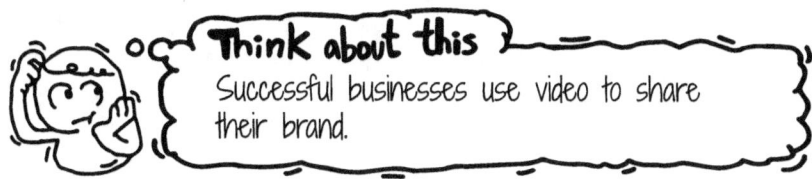

Think about this

Successful businesses use video to share their brand.

I encourage you to let people into the amazing world of the artist. For example, let them see a place they have never been to before. Bring them behind the scenes. You can give them a tour of your studio. People want to see that cool place where the art gets made. They want to peek into the rehearsal hall and see how the performance comes together. You might have a special technique or a process that you can describe or demonstrate. Video is about sharing your world. As an independent artist, we're somewhat isolated when we create our work. I think the best thing you can have on your website is a 'Meet the Artist' section, rather than the usual 'About Me.' Let them see you in your natural, exotic habitat. An 'about' section feels formal. A 'meet me' section is personal. "This is me, this is where I hang out, this is where I make my art." It lets people into your world starts building a relationship with them.

Sharing a time-lapse video of the creation of a piece of visual art, or of the process of loading into the theatre, or setting up for a performance, is very effective. Because again, you are giving people secret access to something that they don't normally get to see.

The best way to share and build your brand is through videos. Get in the habit of creating and sharing lots of video content. Share your likeability and your enthusiasm.

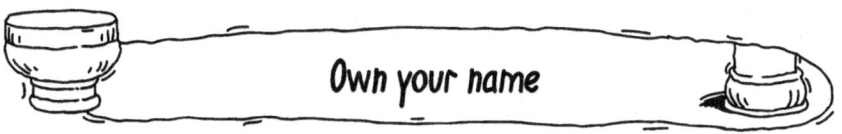

Own your name

I find that a lot of artists hide behind some clever name. Black Door, Random Musings, Jazz Hands, Glass Howz. A clever name just confuses your market. Think about it—your customer has just had a powerful, emotional experience. Your job in branding is to connect that emotional experience back to its source: to you, the artist. They want to remember this amazing artist who has created such an incredible emotional experience for them. When you use some clever business name, you make it harder for them to find you, and they give up trying after a while. They are looking to build a relationship with the artist, but having to remember another business name just gets confusing.

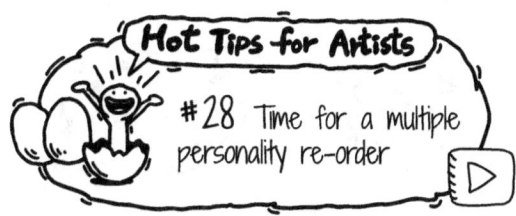

Hot Tips for Artists

#28 Time for a multiple personality re-order

I understand that for some reasons and in some art disciplines, it's important to have a pen name, and that's fine. For example, actors are sometimes forced to have a 'stage name' because their name is already taken by another actor in the business. Or sometimes it is your intention to create an alias like Banksy… but in the main, we recommend using your own name.

Your brand is you, your likeability and your enthusiasm. Find out what your brand is by asking your fans. Start sharing what they say. Share how you do what you do, where you do it, and why you do it in short, sharp video clips. Make sure people are aware of you as the creator of their emotional experience.

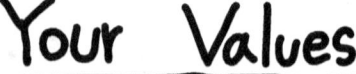

Your Values

As an independent artist, you are not working for someone else. You are in control. You chose this life. You are reading this book because of that choice. You are building a business around it. It's crucial, right now, to make sure that you're in it for the long haul. It's important to know that you're going to be able and willing to do this work for the next twenty years or more. This chapter is about figuring out what's important to you, because you only do what's important to you. You need to build your arts business around your values.

Think about this

You only do what's important to you.

Oftentimes, we find an artist in the middle of their career saying reluctantly, "Yes, I could do that, but I don't like it." Or, "I don't want to do this anymore." Well, if they had created art that was more aligned to their values this wouldn't be the case. You don't want to wake up one day and realise that you are dragging yourself into a business in which you feel trapped into continuing to do something that isn't important to you.

When I talk about values, I mean the things that are important to you. I'm talking about things like integrity, effort, partnership, passion. These are qualities that are part of how you conduct your business. These are things important for your brand and important to you for sustaining your arts business.

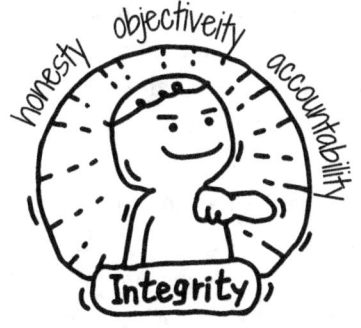

Integrity is an important value for artists in business. You dislike people in the arts who act without integrity. You want to build a business based on honesty and integrity. You also want to maintain objectivity about your business. You want to be a business that stands by your word. You are not one of the 'flaky artists.' You also hold yourself accountable to others and others accountable to you.

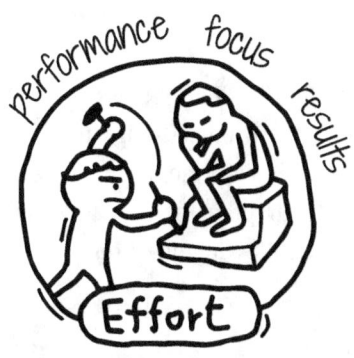

Another value that's important for us as independent artists is effort. You value effort. What comes along with valuing effort is valuing performance. You don't care what people say as much as what they do. Focus is also important. You have intense focus, and you respect others who share this ability. Appreciating results is also an important part of valuing effort. This attitude can be articulated as, "I don't care what you say or do if it doesn't deliver the intended result."

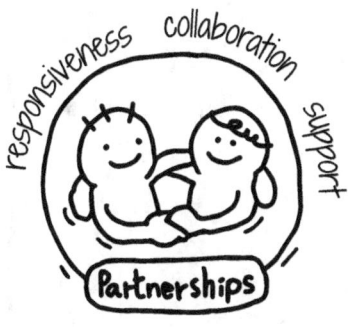

We also value partnership. You create art in partnership with others. You exhibit art in partnership with others. You also create art in partnership with your tools and our medium. Your customers are actually your partners. Being responsive is something you value. You don't like it when someone doesn't get back to you or when you are ignored. Collaboration is also something you value in partnerships. Another thing that's important when you consider the value of partnership is support. If you're going into a relationship that's a partnership, you want to support your partners, and you want your partners to support you.

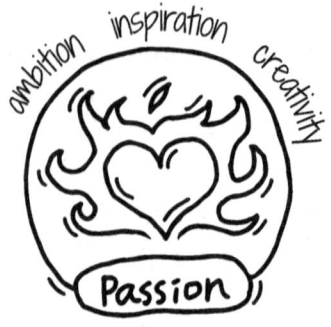

Passion is something that's very important for us. You value ambition, you value inspiration, and you value creativity. These are qualities that you have, and you recognise them in others. You respect the role they play in the creation of your art. Passion must be part of what you want in your arts business. The same ambition that drives your artistic pursuits drives your arts business. You also use inspiration to create your art. The creativity that guides your choices in creating art is the same power that will craft your unique arts business.

What is it that you value? Are **INTEGRITY, EFFORT, PARTNERSHIP** and **PASSION** all things that you value? Are there other things that are important to you as an artist? Are there other values you want to see in your unique arts business? While you're building your pillar of branding and values, this is a great moment to ask yourself the following questions:

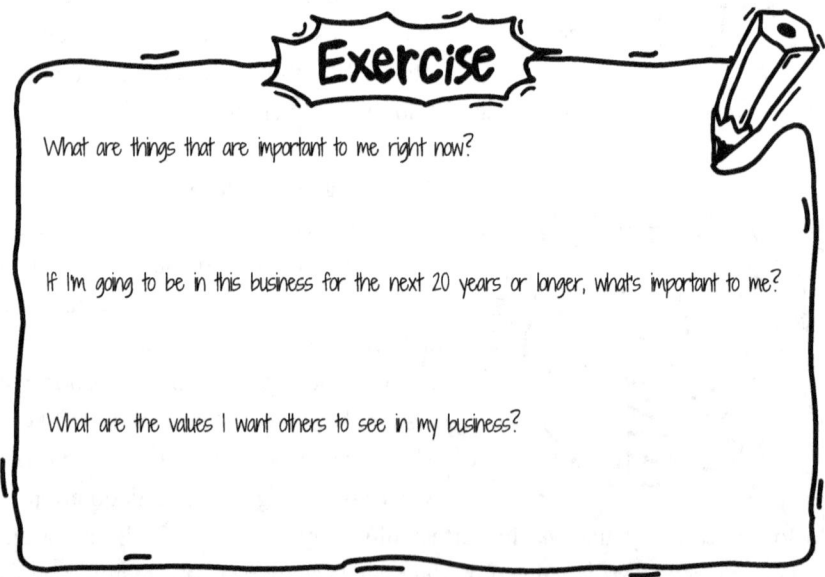

Exercise

What are things that are important to me right now?

If I'm going to be in this business for the next 20 years or longer, what's important to me?

What are the values I want others to see in my business?

Stop and do this exercise. Make a list, and examine the values you write down.

Here's the next question: If these are what you value, how present are they in your thoughts and actions?

Many artists come to work with us because they are experiencing a conflict of values around money. They often say, "I want more money. Making more money is important to me." But the majority of their thoughts and actions are not focused on making money. So, I say, "Well, if you really valued making more money, that's where your thoughts and actions would be. But you know what? When I look at where the value 'making money' shows up in your life, how you spend your time, and where you focus your thoughts, I can see that making money it's really something you value very highly. So let's look at what it is that you really value. Where are your thoughts and your actions focused?" The point of this anecdote is to notice that if making money is important to you, it must show up in what you say and what you do rather than remaining just a wish.

And I think, to get this pillar of Branding & Values right, it's important to have a conversation with fellow artists who are also building businesses or ones who already have successful businesses, and ask them what their values are. What's important to them? Because we only do what's important to us. The things that you value will sustain you and will sustain your business. And when other people come to join you, you can talk about your values, and you can say, "This is what's important to us, this is what's important to me, this is what's important to the group in running this theatre, building this show, creating this art."

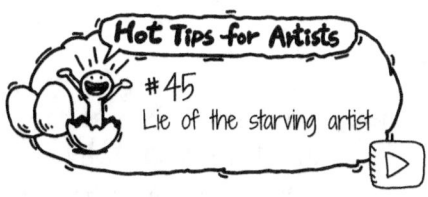

I encourage you to take some time to reflect on your values. Make some lists of values and be on the lookout for where your thoughts are focused. You might have some negative values that are holding your business back. Poverty, workaholism, competition, perfectionism can be values that have a negative result on your business. Being clear about and conscious of your values is the key to sustaining your arts business in the long run. You want to wake up each day eager to create more art. You want each day to be spent doing things that are important to you. When your brand is aligned to your values, you won't have to 'work' a day in your life.

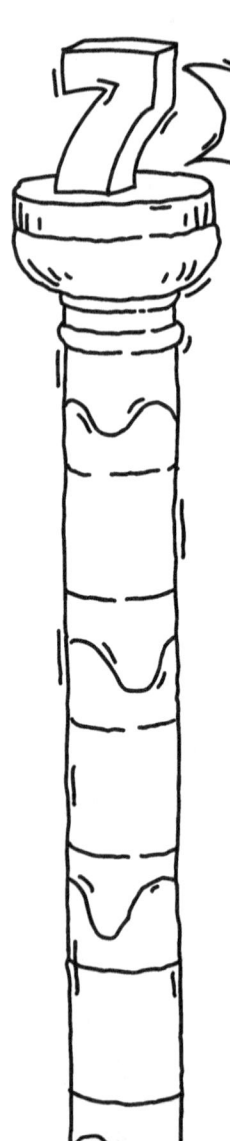

Value your time

I don't know if 'time' made it into the list of things you value, but it definitely needs to be there. You have this one lifetime to create art. How you use your time and how you allow others to use it is critical.

I often say to artists, "When you're offered a contract, or when someone wants to hire you and pay you for your time, ask this question: 'Is this opportunity worth it?' Is it worth your precious, limited time?"

Your time is at your disposal. How you choose to use it is critical to you and your business.

This is especially true for artists. If your time is getting used for things other than creating your products and your services, you're not going to make money from that time. If you do nothing else this week, I want you to start tracking how you use your time. Start valuing your time.

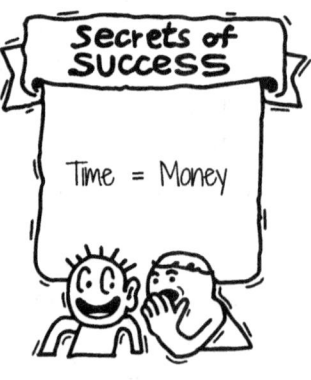

I know that you often hear yourself saying, "I'm so busy," or "Oh, I really want to do that, but I don't have time." Well, you know what? You have the same 24 hours as everyone else. Are you using your time in ways that are important to you and your business? If you're always busy, I ask you, is being busy what is important to you? Is being busy and having all your time used up what you value? I suspect it isn't. You've just allowed this to happen because you haven't been valuing your time.

I tell artists that there are three things you can do: you can sell your time, you can invest your time, and you can spend your time.

You can sell your time.

You know what that means: contracts, hourly gigs, being paid by some measure of time. Knowing that your time is of value, the question you need to ask yourself is, "Are people paying you enough? Is it really worth it for you to spend those 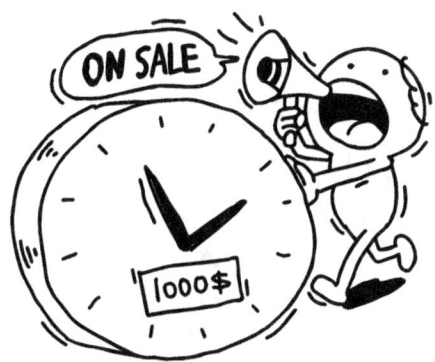 hours doing something for someone else for that amount of money? Is that the best use of your time?" Sometimes the answer is 'yes.' Sometimes the answer is, "I need to make that car payment. I need to save up to buy this piece of equipment." That's fine. I just want the decision to sell your time to be a considered choice. Be really careful about the amount of your time you give away for free. We are often asked for favours or for help. That's OK. Again, just be sure that giving away your time is your choice. Value your time and know that your time is important to you. Make a conscious decision about how you sell your time.

You can invest your time.

And that's by doing things like learning a skill, taking a course, creating something new, or growing your business in some way. You can choose to invest some of your time in your business. Invest it in learning more about your art form. Invest it in exploring. Invest it in trying new things. It's up to you say, "I 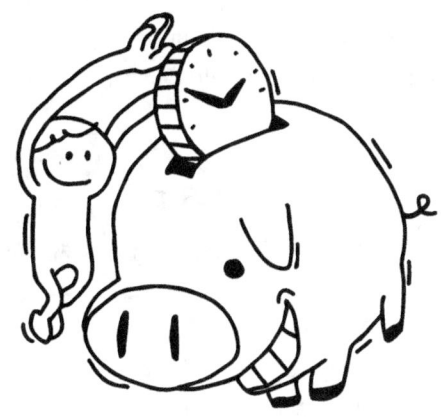 choose to invest this valuable time in growing myself and my business." After all, that's what's really important to you.

You can spend your time.

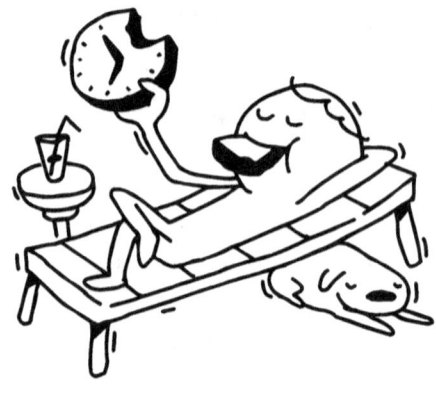

It's your time, so you can choose to spend some of it. You can say, "I'm going to spend this amount of time hanging out with my friends. I'm going to spend this chunk of time to go see a show. I'm going to spend this time to relax. I'm going to spend this time to take a walk in nature. I'm going to spend this time to rejuvenate." You must spend some of your time—you can't always save it for later. Spending time on yourself often gets neglected. If you repeatedly find yourself in the position of not having time to spend, you are headed straight for burnout.

We typically sell too much of our time, so I would encourage you this month to claw back some of the time you sell and invest it in yourself and in your business. I challenge you to block out some time in your diary right now. You're reading this book to grow your business, and that is an investment of your time. Try and reduce the amount of time you're selling, increase the amount of time that you're investing, and make sure that you spend some time on yourself. If you really value your time and you realise how important your time is, then it's up to you to control it. Don't let others control your time. Your time is valuable to you.

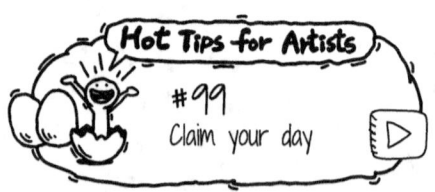

One of my favourite stories of learning to value time comes from an artist we worked with through our Artists Transformation School. She has three teenage boys, and she was always available to them. She was giving her time to them for free. She wasn't consciously choosing to spend her time with them—they were taking her time. The issue became apparent as she started to build her business. I encouraged her to begin to value her time and control it to be able to invest more of it in building her business. She decided to have specific studio hours. She told her family what she wanted, and the best thing happened. Her boys protected that studio time for her. If someone came to bother her, they intercepted them and said, "Nope, mum's in the studio. This is her studio time. You can't have it."

People will learn to adjust if you set the boundaries. They will learn how valuable your time is if you start to control your time. I urge you to value your time. Once you start valuing your time, you'll be able to invest it in your business and spend it on yourself, and that's the whole point.

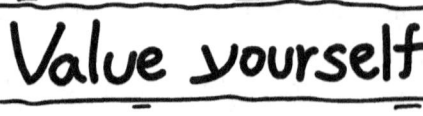

Value yourself

What about valuing yourself? Did 'you' make it on your list of things you value?

Why do you suppose airlines tell you to put your mask on first and then assist other passengers? Because, if you start assisting other passengers without putting on your mask, you collapse and make matters worse for everyone.

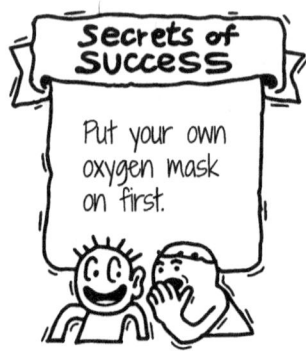

Secrets of Success

Put your own oxygen mask on first.

You are the most important person in your business. The business wouldn't exist without you. The business is built around you, your talent, your abilities, your likeability, and your enthusiasm. If you had a CEO, they would do all kinds of things to care for the most important person in the business. They would make sure you had what you needed and that you were growing. You are your own CEO, so it is up to you to value yourself. No one else is going to do that for you.

You are important. You are the prize. Without you, the next project wouldn't exist. Without you, the current opportunity wouldn't exist. If someone wants an amazing emotional experience, you are the one who can create it.

I encourage you to learn to say "No." If someone does not value you, makes you an offer that will waste your time and waste your energy, say "No." Pause and ask yourself, "Is this person or this offer worth my time, my energy, and my love? Am I going to grow from this? Is this going to feed my soul? Is this going to help me develop in some way?" After reading the last chapter, you've begun valuing your time, so you say, "I could make better use of that time by spending it on something that's important to me, such as investing it in my business." When you value yourself and realise that your time, your energy, and your soul are important, it's easier for you to say "No" because it is in your best interest to do so.

Your talent is sometimes taken for granted by yourself and by others around you. You sometimes value other's needs above your own. You could paint, rehearse, choreograph, write or compose at some other time, simply because it's easy to do so. It's just your God-given talent. Others notice this behaviour, and you find yourself in a situation where you are taking care of others' needs all the time. You are busy doing things for them. This diagram depicts how your life tends to feel.

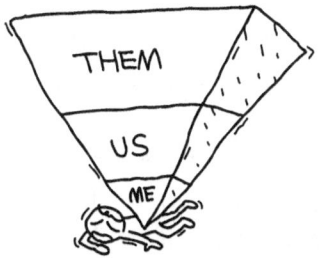

THEY acquire a lot of importance and value. THEY ask for your energy, your art, your creativity, and your time. And you're so busy doing things for THEM that there's hardly any time and energy left to build and nurture US. And by 'US', I mean your partners and your close family. After you've met the needs of THEM and US, it's only a matter of time before that tiny little ME at the bottom of the pyramid, who's trying to hold it all together, collapses.

Reverse this dynamic. Flip this pyramid to the way it is supposed to be to create a sustainable arts business as well as a sustainable life.

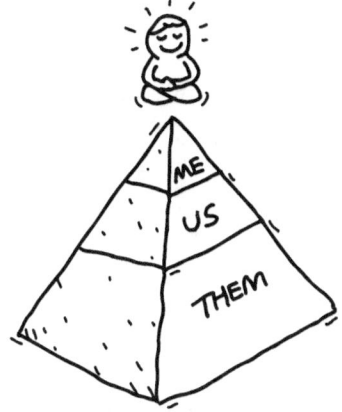

Start at the top with taking care of the ME part. You are the energy source for your arts business. When you see yourself as the valuable top of this pyramid, as the most valuable element of your art and your business, you become better and stronger. When you are healthier and stronger, everything beneath you becomes stronger and better too. When there's more of ME to nurture US, then there's more of US to nurture all of THEM. It is not you alone who are responsible for US and THEM. You are responsible for ME, for valuing ME, and for making ME the most important person in your life.

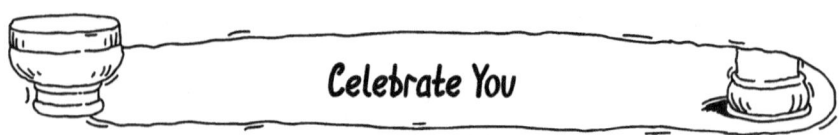

Celebrate You

Remember that as an independent artist, you are the boss. There is no boss to congratulate you or to give you the 'atta-boy' or the 'atta-girl' pat on the back. But you still deserve recognition and the reward. If you don't reward yourself, don't salute yourself, don't value the extraordinary contribution you just made, who will?

When was the last time you celebrated your success? What was the last reward you gave yourself for a job well done? When you create something beautiful, achieve something extraordinary, 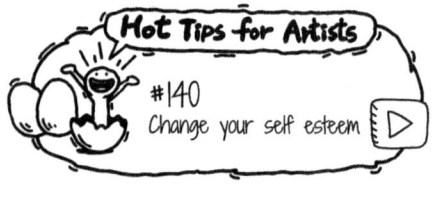 control your time, manage your money, or succeed in small or large ways, it's important to reward yourself. When a positive action gets rewarded, your subconscious mind says, "Oh, that felt good. Let's do more of that."

I bet your calendar is full of things to do. I would also bet that there's nowhere on your calendar blocked out for your reward. As artists, we just stay busy, and then we drop. We pause, we rest, we recuperate, and then we get busy again. Let's stop that pattern. Value your time, value yourself, and reward the most important person in this business for achievements and positive behaviour.

Let's look at this little exercise.

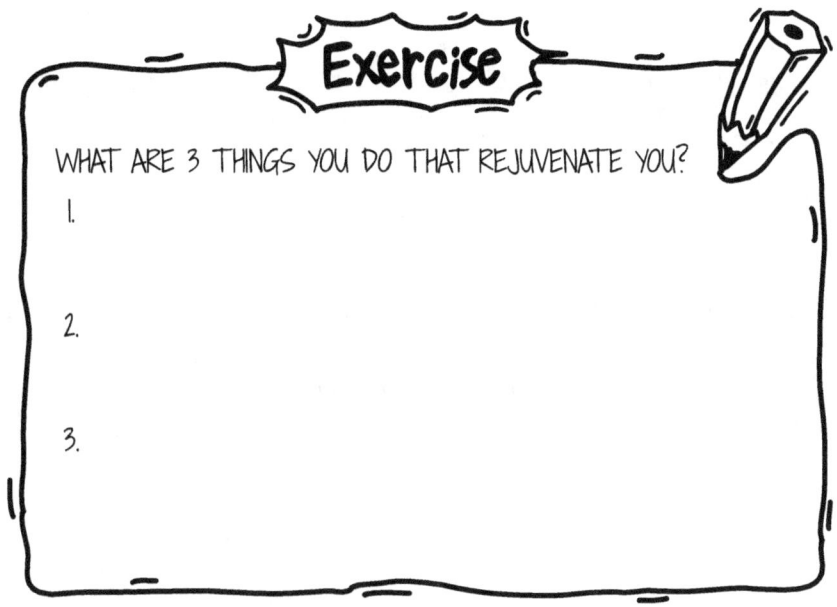

WHAT ARE 3 THINGS YOU DO THAT REJUVENATE YOU?

1.

2.

3.

In the box, I want you to write down three things you do that rejuvenate you.

The next step is to schedule them in your calendar right now.

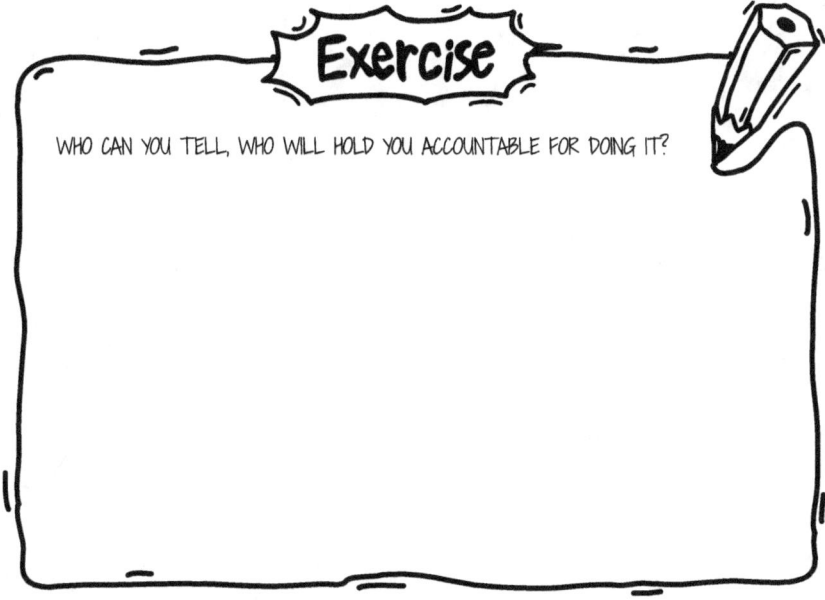

WHO CAN YOU TELL, WHO WILL HOLD YOU ACCOUNTABLE FOR DOING IT?

Now, find a buddy who can celebrate your success with you. Book time in your diary for those three activities so that you start to reward yourself. And if someone is going to join you in this reward, I want you to text them right now. Ask, "Are you available to celebrate with me?" They're going to reply, "Of course, I'll come celebrate with you. What are we celebrating?" That's your opportunity to value yourself and talk about what you've just done and share your success with someone who you love and who cares about you.

I think you can feel why it's important to value yourself. I hope you realise that you are the prize. I hope you spend next week looking at ways you can be kind to yourself, value yourself, reward yourself, and treat yourself like the most important person in your arts business, because you are.

Story of Success

Trudy Rice

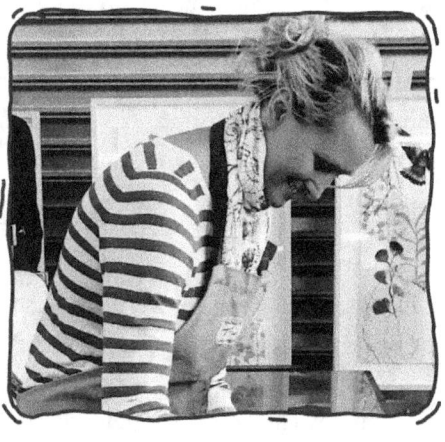

I'd like to introduce you to an incredible visual artist, teacher, and printmaker. Trudy Rice completed the Artists Transformation School with us. At the end of the intense 12-week program, she decided to hold a solo exhibition as an opportunity to implement all the things she learned in the course. For the first time, she confidently took the stage and talked about her art, her inspiration, and her process of printmaking. She established her brand. She didn't hide behind the curator of the gallery—she realised that she was the most important person in her business, and her brand was important enough for her to step up. She sold 23 of the 40 pieces exhibited. She exchanged business cards, and now has two high-profile interior designers who recommend her work. She also has representation for licensing her designs. All this success came because she put her brand forward. She explained what she did. She shared why she did it. She took people into the process. She shared her inspiration and her enthusiasm for nature.

In the three months following the course, she has actually doubled her income, and for the first time, she's also getting paid for the work she used to do for free. She's the artist with the three teenage boys I told you about, and her career is fabulous. Her business is incredibly exciting. She told us that understanding her brand, valuing her time, and valuing herself made it possible for her business to take off. She said that she's sold more work in the last four months than she had since the middle of last year. That's the power of her business, her brand, and her values. What's important to Trudy is nature and the patterns of plants, animals, and birds. She combines those patterns in ways that are inspiring and beautiful and that resonates with lots of her customers.

I'm not telling you about Trudy's success to blow my own horn, but so that you see that you can achieve it too, once you sort out your brand and your values. Running your arts business is about knowing who you are and why people love you and aligning that knowledge with what you care about in the world. Valuing yourself and your time makes this second pillar so strong that it can support your growth and the growth of your business.

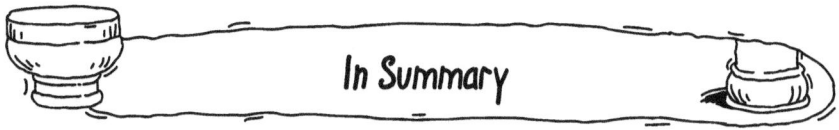

In Summary

Sorting out your Branding & Values identifies you and your art as distinct in the marketplace. Building your brand around what your market appreciates about you means that you have a strong connection between what you offer and what your customers want. You are going to be an artist creating great art for a long time. It is critical that you ensure that there is agreement between what you think you are about and what your customers think you are about.

A sustainable arts business is one that is aligned with what is important to you. If you go to work each day to create work that is aligned to your values, it will never feel like 'work.' People are going to want to help an artist when they personally align with your big 'WHY.'

Let people get to know you. Share your enthusiasm and your likeability. The very best way to share yourself and why you do what you do is by creating video content. Don't let your perfectionism stand in the way of shooting some short videos.

Make the decision right now to start valuing your time and yourself. Part of valuing your time and yourself is to make sure that you are taken care of. As your business gets more successful, you must be a good CEO and take care of your most important team member, yourself, 'the artist'. Find that friend who will celebrate your achievements with you. Spend the time you need to rejuvenate and recharge. A burnt-out artist is no good to anyone. Your likeability and enthusiasm will diminish, and you will hurt your brand and violate your values.

Don't move on to the next chapter without taking some action in the next 48 hours.

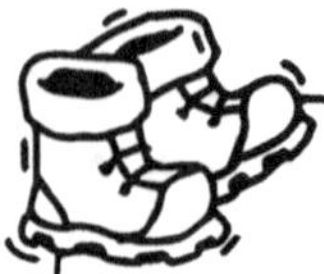

Exercise

BRANDING&VALUES

where to from here:
(Do something in the next 48 hours or you won't ever.)

- Something that hit home for me in this section is:

  _____

- 3 things I need help with:

  _____

  _____

  _____

- The one thing I'm going to do to get my branding and values sorted is:

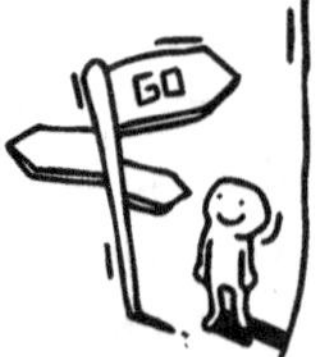

  _____

Artists before you have identified these top six things from this section as worthy of their focus:

1. What is my brand?

2. What is the benefit of my art?

3. Make 30 second videos that share 'me.'

4. Name my values.

5. Value my time.

6. Value myself.

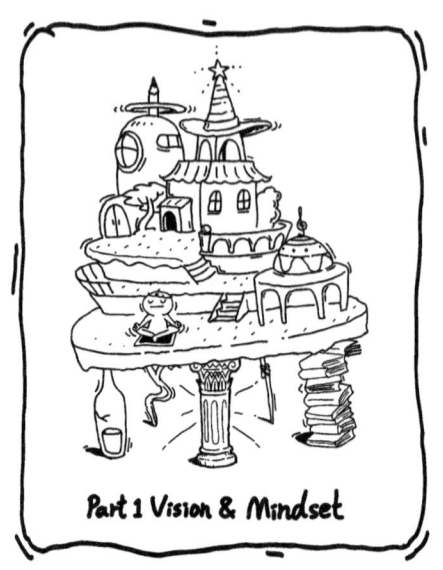

Part 1 Vision & Mindset

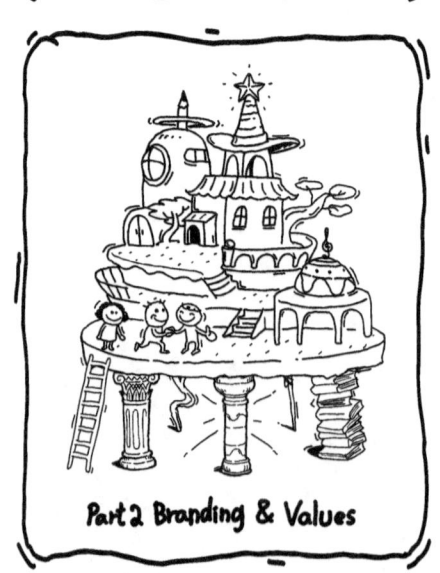

Part 2 Branding & Values

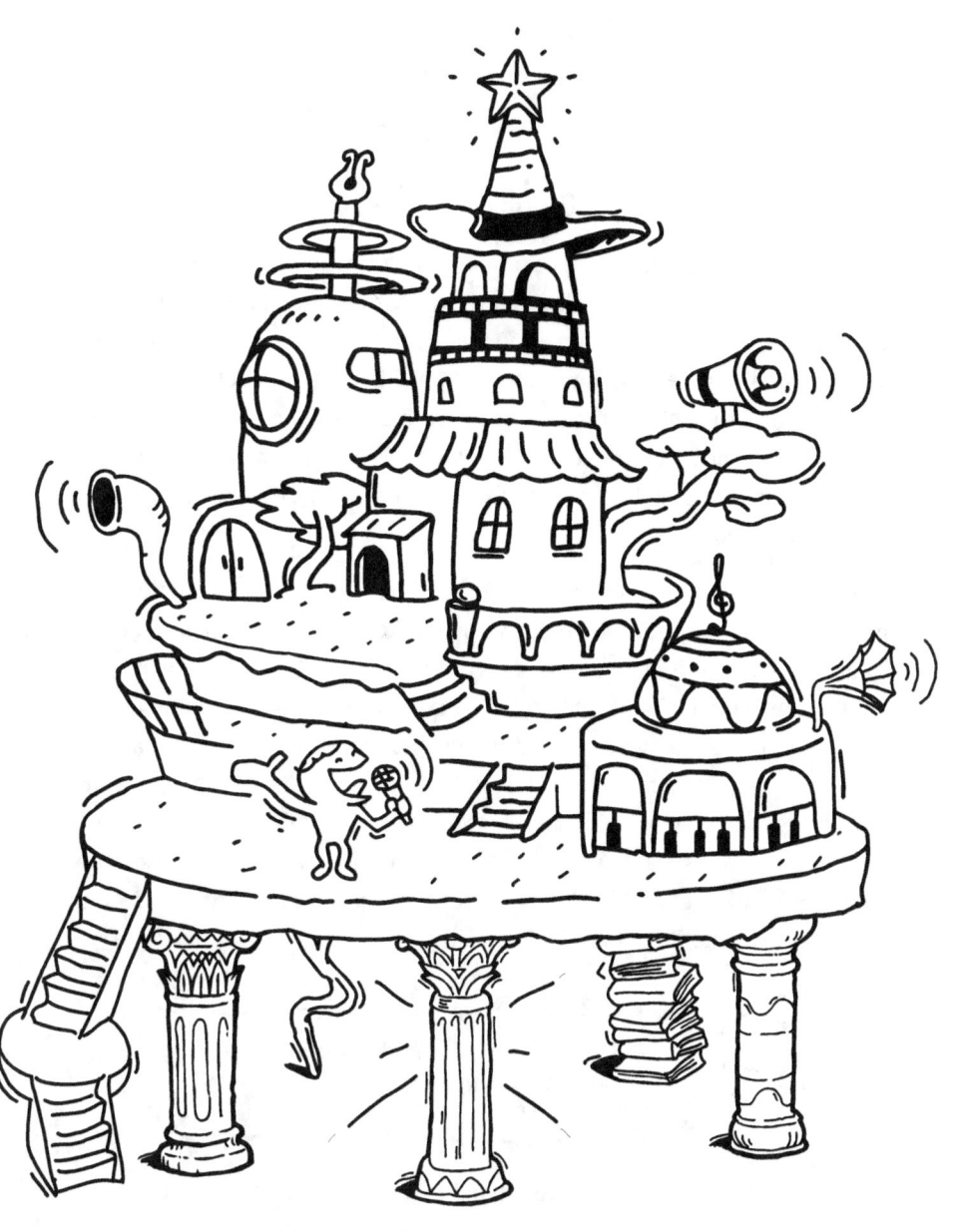

Part 3 Marketing & Message

To build the third strong pillar of your arts business, you need to answer these questions to ensure that you are building a sustainable business.

Who are your customers?
Why do they want you?

It's time to send out your message to your market: who you are, why you do what you do, and how your products and services meet their need for awesome emotional experiences. Remember, in the previous section I showed you the model of small businesses: a market plus a need, and a product or a service. The most important thing for you to figure out is the emotional need you meet with your artistic products and services. When it comes to marketing and advertising, your job is merely to communicate a clear message about the need you meet.

Before we go any further, I want to make sure that we are clear about the term 'marketing.' There's a difference between marketing and advertising. I refer to marketing as the strategy and process of finding people who need what you have to offer. Market-ing is finding the market. Marketing is communicating with people in various ways to find the people who want what you have to offer. When you find a market that might be suitable for your art, part of your job is to figure out what their needs are and to determine if your product or your service satisfies them. Once that is confirmed, advertising is simply letting that market know that you and your art exist and where, when, and how to get the benefit they are looking for.

Think about this
Marketing is finding the market. Advertising is letting them know that your product or service meets their need.

As a small arts business, we recommend that you spend 30% of your time and 20% of your budget on marketing and advertising. If you work in your arts business 40 hours per week, 12 hours need to be spent on finding your market, growing your market, and advertising to them. If your new project has a budget, then 20% of that budget should be spent on marketing and advertising activities.

Let's head out and build this third pillar, Marketing & Message.

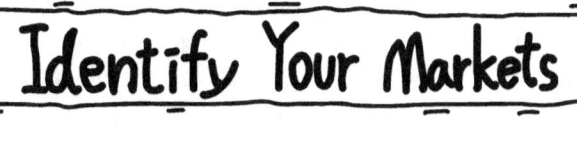

Identify Your Markets

To find and grow your market, figure out who 'gets' you and loves what you do.

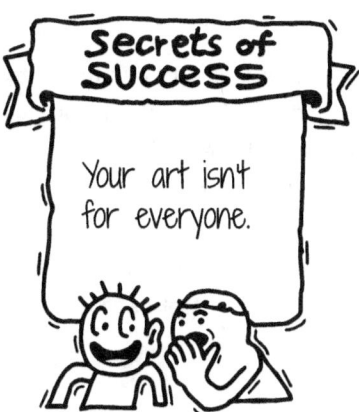

Too many artists don't know who their market is. This a consequence of the way we build arts businesses (creating the product or service first). You've created some cool work, but you don't know who's going to like it the most. Your art isn't for everyone. However, your art is ideally suited for some specific market, and that's called your niche market.

Figure out who your niche market is so that you can focus on them. They are connected to people outside the niche, and they can translate your value into language that their friends, who are not in the niche, might understand. It's too hard for you to imagine all the different ways to describe the benefits and the value of your art to people outside the niche. It is much easier for you to explain the value and the benefits of your art to people inside your niche.

The other question I often ask artists is, "Who will get it the most?" Who's going to absolutely understand, feel, appreciate, and desire your art? Once you know who your niche market is, you can find more people who belong to it. You may have a couple of different niche markets for your artistic products or services.

While it's good to understand the needs of the niche who will directly receive the emotional experience of your art, you might have another type of customer at the same time. You may be in a situation where you need to be aware of the needs of a gallery curator or a venue programmer. If you have someone who acts as a 'broker' for you and your art, they are looking for different benefits and have different needs. You need to develop marketing collateral that is different for them.

Now that you realise that knowing your niche markets is a good thing, and that sometimes a broker might have different needs, it's time to create your customer avatars.

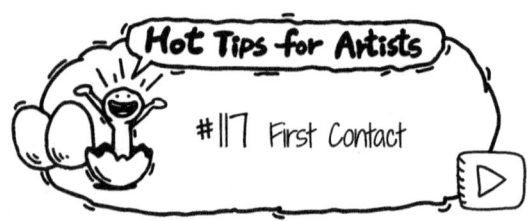

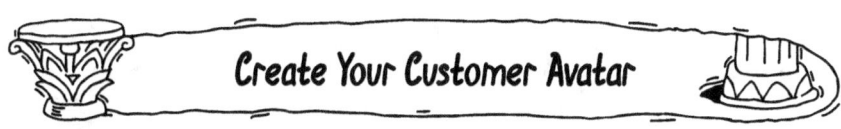

Create Your Customer Avatar

If you figure out who will love your art product or service the most, you can find more of them.

You might have different avatars for every one of your products or services. You will have an avatar for the person who directly experiences your art. You will also have an avatar for the brokers who give you access to your direct market—curators, festival producers, agents, casting directors, venue managers, journalists, funders. You can use this exercise for each of your products by creating one customer avatar for the person who ultimately experiences your art and a different customer avatar for your 'broker.'

To build an avatar, get into your avatar's shoes. Use your powerful imagination and imagine this person. What do they want? What do they need? What's the value that they're hoping you and your art will deliver?

Pick one of your products or services and imagine the ideal customer, either your 'broker' or your direct customer. Use the full power of your imagination and give them a name. For example, let's decide that Sarah is a direct customer. She interacts with you directly to experience you art. On this first chart, you're going to imagine her demographics. Yes, you're making this up. Trust your intuition to build this demographic profile.

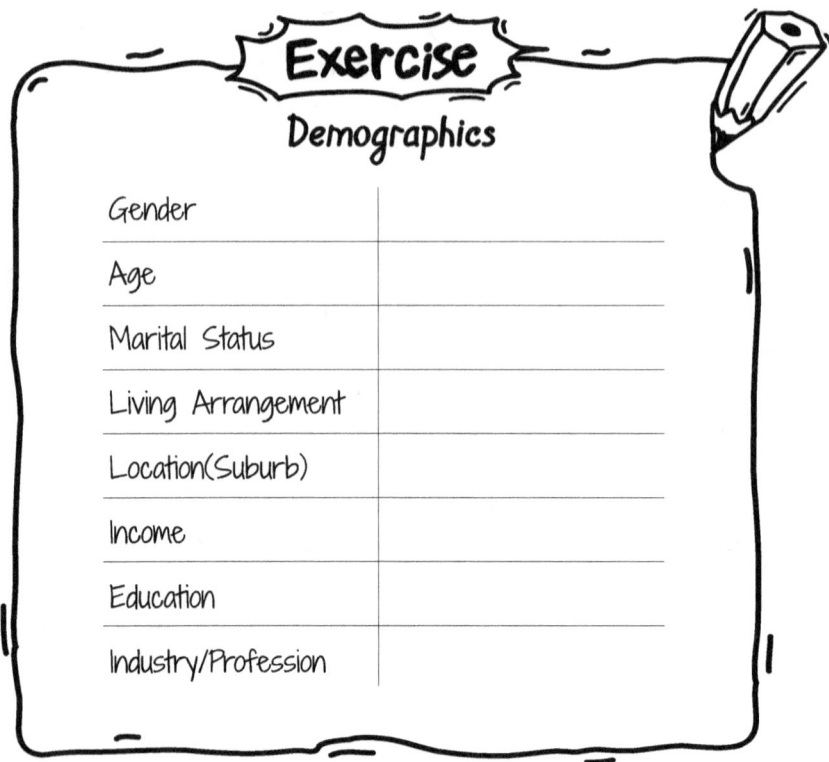

Exercise

Demographics

Gender

Age

Marital Status

Living Arrangement

Location(Suburb)

Income

Education

Industry/Profession

The next section helps you flesh out your avatar by looking at psychographics.

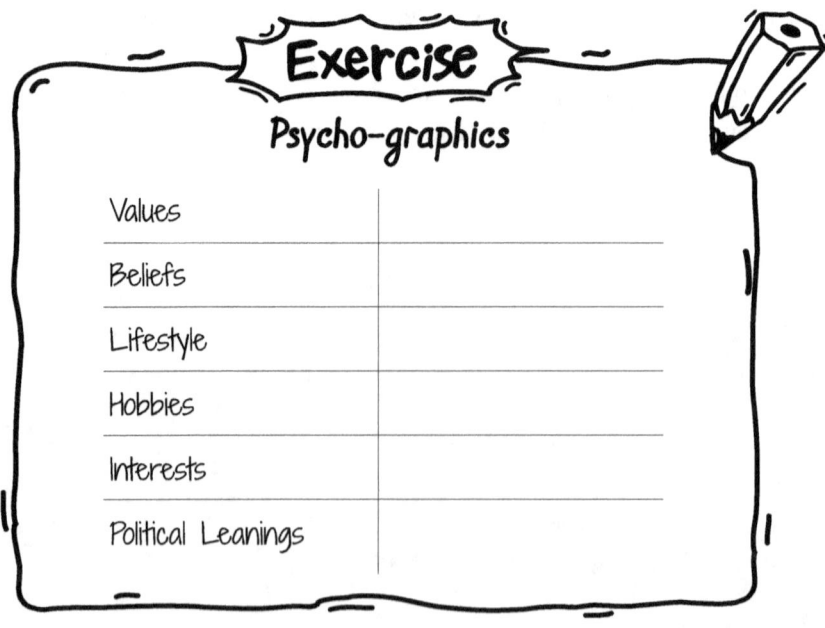

Exercise

Psycho-graphics

Values

Beliefs

Lifestyle

Hobbies

Interests

Political Leanings

Then you're going to complete the character sketch.

Exercise

Character Sketch

Where do they eat

_____

What are they wearing
(where do they shop)

_____

what movie did thy just see

_____

What TV shows do they watch

_____

What Social Media do they use

_____

Where do they hang out

_____

This is the most powerful marketing exercise that an artist can do. For example, if Sarah values nature, cares about climate change, and does yoga, the best place to exhibit your work or put out flyers about your show would be at yoga studios or at organic food shops. Once you construct an avatar, you can figure out how to find more people like her. You need to use your precious advertising dollars on things that will reach your avatar. Stop wasting money on advertising that we call 'spray and pray.' That's putting postcards everywhere, putting up posters up all over town, and trying to market to everyone and anyone. It is way cheaper to get your art in front of a well-targeted avatar.

> Get in the mind, spirit and heart of your customer.

Your avatar is someone who's going to love you the most, who's going to get what you do. Build your avatars, and then grow your markets by finding more of them.

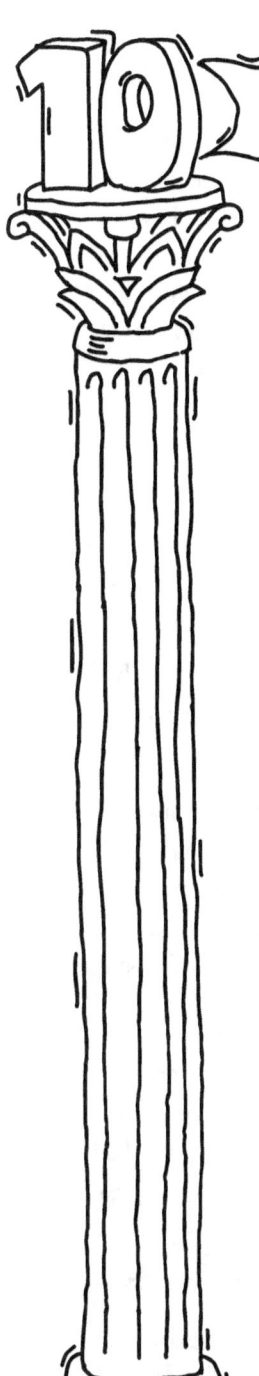

Sharing not Selling

You're going to make some profound shifts in the way you communicate your business as you build this pillar, Marketing & Message. You are going to switch from creating marketing messages that focus on selling to marketing messages that focus on sharing instead. As artists, we are typically not very good at sales. We're too far on the inside the art to be good at sales. It's far easier to sell someone else's art, isn't it? When the thing we are trying to sell is something we've created, we lack the external perspective required for effective selling.

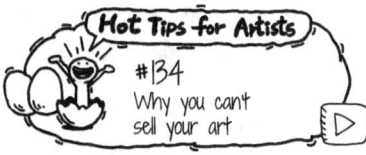

Hot Tips for Artists
#134
Why you can't
sell your art

To be able to view your work as your customer would view it and identify the benefits and the value of your art is an important skill to cultivate. Until you hone this skill, focus on sharing your work, sharing your creative process, and sharing your motivation for creating it.

The truth of sales is

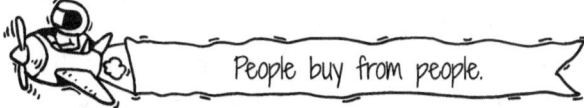

People buy from people.

You are building relationships, not just taking people's money and running. Start building relationships by sharing.

It's your obligation to help your art get out there. "But the art should speak for itself!" you might say. Bullshit! The art cannot speak for itself. It does not have vocal chords. It cannot write its own copy. Speaking for your art—that too is your job. You owe it to your art. The easiest way for you to do that is to share. Take the pressure off selling and just share.

Start talking about your passion. Your 'why' is where people will connect with you. Share what motivates you. Share what inspires you.

You can also share your triumphs. When you get accepted into a show or book a concert gig, share that. Share your enthusiasm and your excitement. Share what this means to you and why it's important to you. When you share your triumphs, it's a quick little bit of pull marketing. Your fans will think, "Oh, wow! How great! You got into XYZ." When they google XYZ, that's pull marketing.

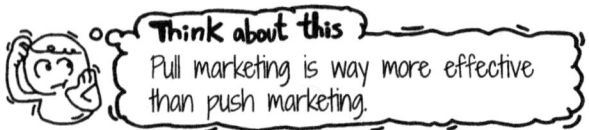

Think about this
Pull marketing is way more effective than push marketing.

When you share something of interest and value to your potential customers, they're going to pull more information. Having them take action is the goal of your marketing message. When they take any action, they are two to three times more likely to buy your product or service. Pull marketing happens when you share something.

Social media is the place for sharing. It is not the place for pushing. Oftentimes, I see visual artists who post the finished painting on social media and leave it at that. Continually pushing finished products is not smart. That's not sharing anything. Don't reveal the whole painting on social media. Use pull marketing to make them curious to see the final product on your website.

Find some exciting moments to share throughout the creation process. We worked with a ceramic artist who realised the power of sharing the process. She created videos of loading the kiln, and then did a live Facebook event of opening the kiln once it had cooled and revealing the magic that had happened. People responded and asked to buy her products. She didn't push them—they asked. Sharing creates pull marketing that builds relationships and leads to sales.

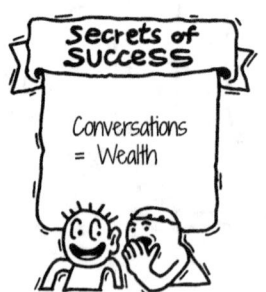

Secrets of Success

Conversations = Wealth

If you're not having any conversations about yourself and your art, there will be no wealth. Stop believing that the gallery or the agent will do all the talking. You're the best person to talk about what you're creating.

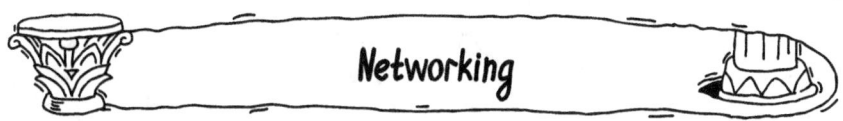

Networking

Most artists hate networking. Most of us are a mix of introvert and extrovert. We put our art out in the world in the manner of an extrovert, and we also like to spend our time alone or with a very small, intimate group of friends. You know that you have an obligation to help get your art out into the world. Networking is part of running a successful arts business.

Often networking triggers anxiety, because you don't know what to say when someone innocently asks, "What do you do?" You stammer and stutter and end up telling them way too much about everything you do. That's overwhelming for the listener.

Consider this: You have an amazing array of bright sparkly gems inside you. In that anxious moment when someone asks you what you do, you vomit up all your gems, spewing out an overwhelming amount of shininess.

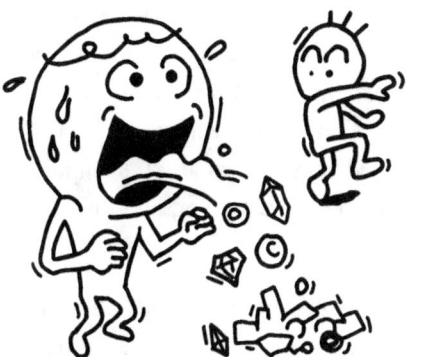

They have no idea which gem to be interested in, or which gem to talk about. So, before you disgorge all your amazing creativity, adopt this networking habit. Ask questions and listen. Don't focus on trying to impress. When you meet someone new, be the first person to speak, "Hi, my name is John Paul. What's the reason you came here today?"

Be the person to ask first. Then, be a good listener. You're looking for someone who fits your customer avatar profile or has access to those people. If they fit, then you can talk about the needs you meet, and then they will ask you to share what you do that meets that need. They will pull the information from you about the shiny artistic gem they are interested in.

You will find it very refreshing to take the pressure off trying to be an expert at sales and focus on how you can be smarter and more effective at sharing.

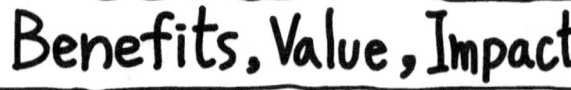

Benefits, Value, Impact

As you construct more of your pillar of Marketing & Message, it's important to understand that your messages need to be about benefits, value, and impact. Describe the value and the benefits more than you describe the actual product or service. This is a challenge for us. We were never taught to promote the impact of our products, to describe the benefit that our product or service delivers, and to share the value of our artistic practice. But this is the key to building a business.

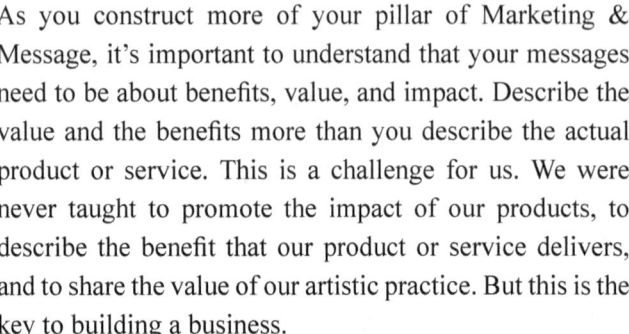

Talk less about your product or service.
Talk more about the benefits, value and impact.

Once you realise the benefits, the value, and the impact of your artistic product or service, you will sell more, because your market wants that. Once you know what emotional benefit they want, for example happiness, you can create pieces and experiences that generate happiness. That's easy, because it's aligned to your values. It's important to you. It's what your brand is known for, and that's why people love you.

Understanding the benefits, the value, and the impact of your work is not an easy job, because you are on the inside. You're the creator. You're not the consumer of your artistic product and service. So, you need to ask your customers. You need to be in dialogue with them. Learn to feel comfortable asking your fans about the benefits they receive from your art, about its value, about why you're important to them. Ask them directly about the impact your work has on them. Whatever they tell you is going to give you the words to use for your message as you reach out and share your work.

Lots of other industries have switched their marketing messages to value-based language years ago, because it works. Yet they struggle to find the impact and the value of particular objects they manufacture. We, on the other hand, create emotional experiences. We open hearts, we stretch minds, and we change lives every time we produce art. Your products and services have an immediate impact on people. You

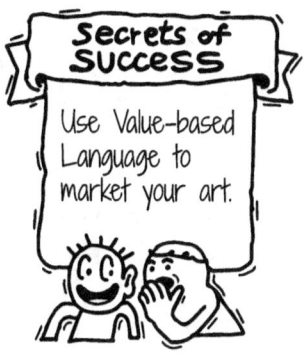

deliver heaps of value. You just have to identify the benefits, the value, and the impact of your art. Ask your customers, scoop up what they say, and start using that language. Value-based marketing and advertising language talks about **what's in it for them.**

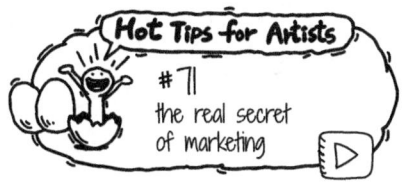

Talk passionately and specifically about the benefits, the value, and the impact of your art to your market.

Copywriting is not essay writing. In school, we were all taught essay writing: introduction, body, conclusion. Unfortunately, many artists still use this for their marketing. It doesn't work. No one has the time to read your essay.

To create good marketing copy using value-based language, start with the conclusion. If you produce a video, don't save the best moments for the end. What your market wants is impact. When your most exciting image is at the end of your video, after 90 seconds, no one is going to be there to see it. Move the thing that people want, the thing that has the most impact, to the first line of text and the first 4 seconds of your video. Change your message right now. Share the value and the benefit rather than showing the product or the service.

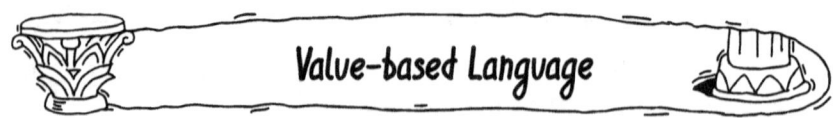

Value-based Language

To embrace value-based language and use it effectively, you need to be able to answer this question, "What are the benefits of my art?" And you're going to determine that by asking your fans and your followers. What is the benefit they receive from your art? What happens to them intellectually, emotionally, and spiritually? You're in the emotion business and emotion is connected to thoughts, right? You are asking them to think about their emotional experience of your art. Their thoughts create feelings, and feelings create behaviour and actions…

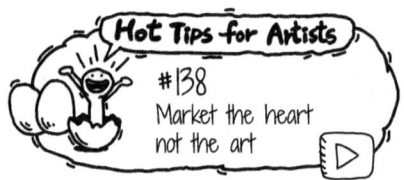

Hot Tips for Artists

#138
Market the heart
not the art

Once you figure out what emotion your customers feel, you can figure out the thoughts that come before that emotion and create marketing messages that trigger those thoughts. Then you can figure out the actions that you want resulting from that emotion. Then help your customers take that step. It takes practice to identify the benefits of your art. As you get more and more experienced at marketing, you'll get better at value-based language. You'll start to hear similar things from your customers. You'll begin to recognise patterns and phrases they use to describe your value, impact, and benefits.

Start asking your customers. Whatever they tell you can be used in crafting your value-based messages. Look back at the exercise in Chapter 5: Why do people spend their time and money on you? If you know the answers and have evidence, then that's the benefit, that's the impact, and that forms part of the message of your value-based language.

Becoming proficient with value-based language will take practice and time. We typically work with artists across six months to develop their value-based language muscles. The lasting benefit of using value-based language is that it builds relationships based on trust.

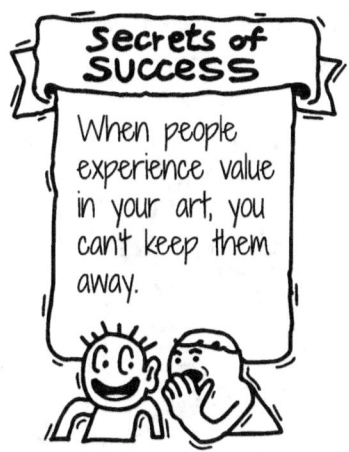

Secrets of Success

When people experience value in your art, you can't keep them away.

In crafting your messages to grow your market, the most important shift you can make is to figure out what your customer recognises as the benefit, then deliver value, and thus create impact.

12) E-marketing and the Customer Journey

The internet and social media have made it possible for us to be in direct contact with our customers. It's easy for our customers to find out more about us. Your customer goes on a journey from the point of discovering that you exist, to engaging with you, purchasing some of your art, and sharing it with their friends. You can use e-marketing and social media to make it easy for your customers to make the customer journey.

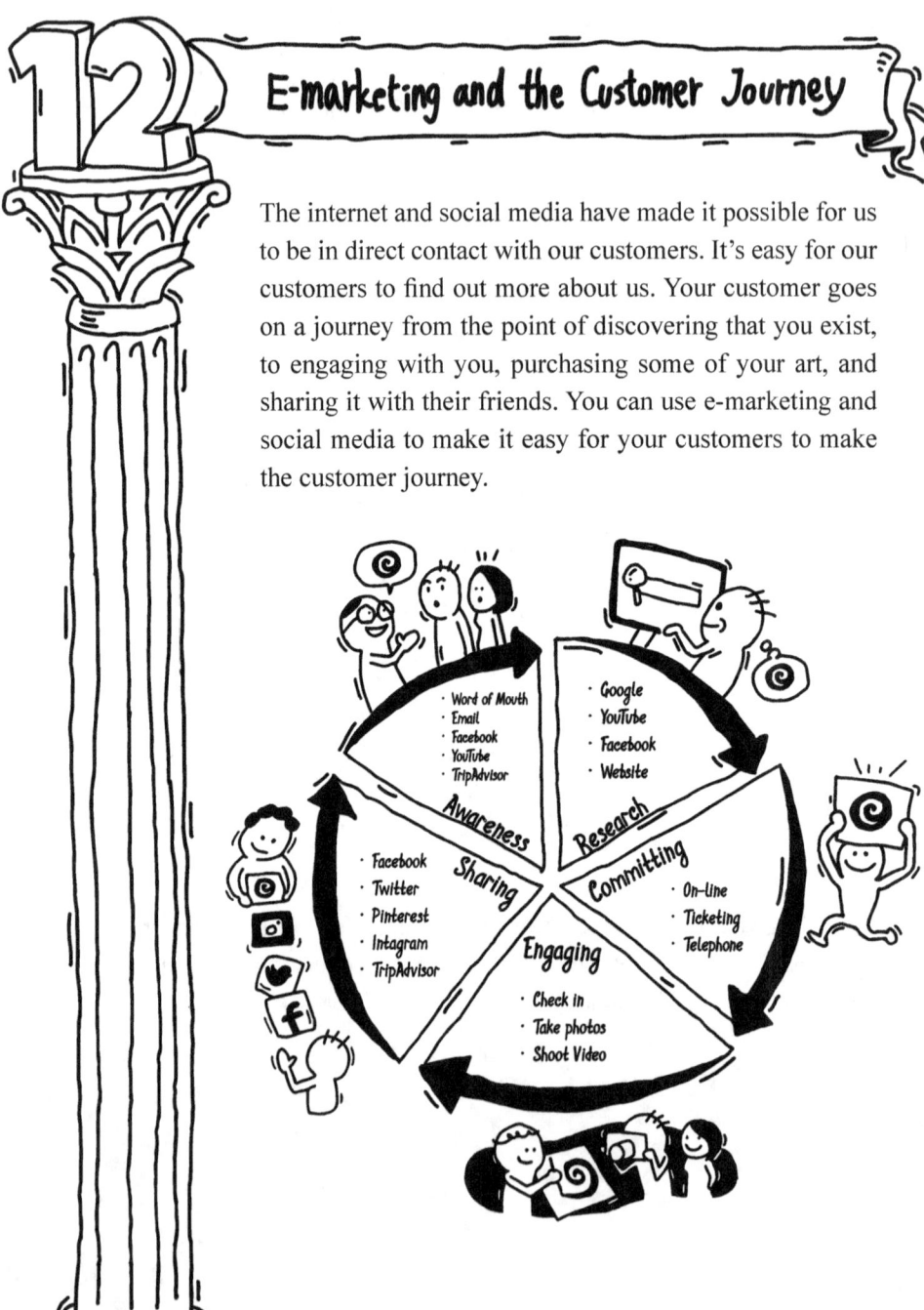

The journey starts with awareness.

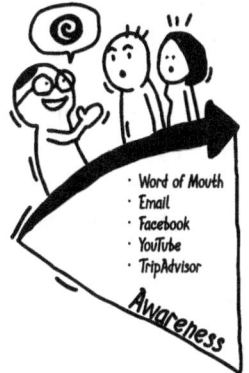

Your customers find out that you exist. Typically, this happens by word of mouth. They find out from someone they know that there's an artist delivering great emotional impact. Someone they trust likes you, has experienced some of your work, and supports you and tells them about you. This often happens online, on social media. Someone takes a selfie at your exhibition, or at your show, or at your concert, and posts it on Instagram, or they share a post on Facebook that says, "I just went to this awesome concert." They share the benefits and the value they got from the experience. Sometimes it happens in an email. "Hey, I just had this really cool experience. I think you'd really like it." They endorse you. They promote you to a friend. Or it could be through a text message or, in the case of visual art, through an Instagram post of some of your work.

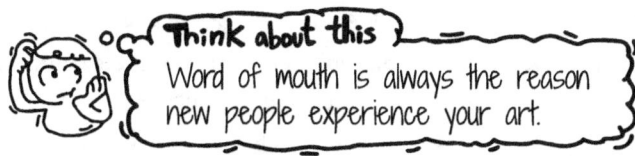

Somewhere on social media, information about you has travelled by word of mouth. Your customer has shared the emotional impact of your work. Because of that 'word of mouth' share, you have new potential customers, new members of your market who suddenly become aware of you, and that begins their customer journey.

Then they're going to do some research.

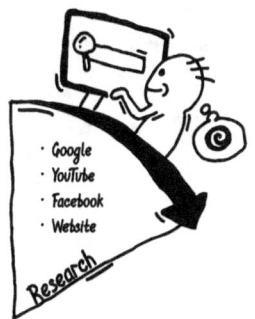

From simply being aware of you, these people are now going to do some research. Their research typically happens online as well. They might talk to their friend and pull more information about you. But ultimately, at some point, they're going to want their own relationship with you and your brand. At least they are going to investigate the possibility of a relationship with you. They are going to do some research themselves to find out more about you and your art. They are going to type in your name on Google, because you are the person who delivered the emotional benefit they have heard about. They may only know the name of the theatre or gallery where your work has been exhibited. They are trying to find you, the person, the artist who generated that emotional experience and delivered the value they heard about.

When they google your name, what are they going to find? Are they going to find you? Make it easy for them. Make sure you do a little bit of SEO (search engine optimisation) work. Make sure that you own your name on all platforms, so that when they try to find out about you, they can.

The other place they're going to look for you is YouTube. YouTube is the second largest search engine. Make sure that your YouTube channel pops up when they run a search. Make sure there are videos that share who you are, what you do, and why you do what you do. That's the information they are looking for. Make sure that if they look for you on Facebook, they find your artist's page. And of course, they're going to end up on your actual website. Make sure that your website is designed to answer their questions. So many artists' websites are just fancy portfolios of their work. That's not using value-based language. Those websites are only pushing what you want to say. Not effective! You're in business. You've read this book. Your website needs to be built from the point of view, "What do they want to know?" What is the person accessing your website trying to find, trying to discover, trying to learn about? In this second phase of the customer journey, your customer has only just become aware of you, and now they have three questions:

Make sure that on social media and online, you answer these questions.

If their research is successful, and they find that you're a likeable person, and that you're enthusiastic, and that you're good, and that your information is current, then **they're going to move to the next stage of committing.**

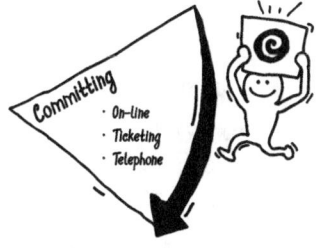

Committing might involve doing something like signing up for your newsletter, liking your page on Facebook, RSVP-ing to your event, or following you on Instagram. They're going to commit to forming a relationship. This phase of the customer journey happens mostly online. Those of you who are in the performing arts will will find new customers committing to their work when they buy tickets. They're going to give your work a try. This third phase in the customer journey is about making the commitment to form a relationship with you.

After they form this relationship with you, there's an opportunity for them to engage with you.

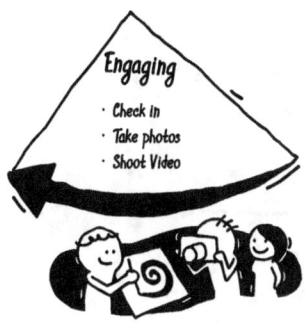

They come to your exhibition, they come to your performance. They engage directly, personally, with you and your art. At this stage, it's very important that you acknowledge their engagement. Physically, welcome them. Let them check in or even sign in. Let them take photos. Let them shoot a video if they want to. Acknowledge the fact that they have engaged with you and your art. You engage with art every day of your life. The average person who is not an artist engages with art as a rare, exciting, and occasional experience. Help them to engage more fully. You might send them email messages in advance that help them understand your art. Your new customer has chosen to engage. Please don't ignore them. Recognise that they have chosen to spend their time and their money on you, and value them back. Let them enjoy the full value of engaging with you and your art.

Once they've engaged with you and your art, they've received most of the value and the benefits you offer. The impact has been made, so they want to share it, and they move into the next phase: the sharing phase of the customer journey.

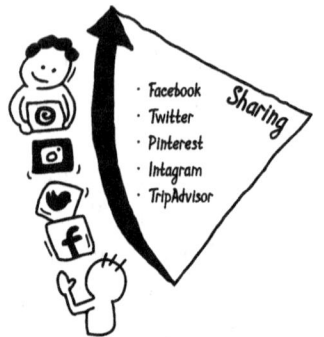

Your customer is going to share their experience. A recent study of arts consumers discovered that eighty-seven percent of people who experience art share their experience within 48 hours. They're going to send messages by email, by text, and in person. They're going to use social media to share. Make sure they can connect the emotional experience they just had back to you, the source. People share because they want their friends to receive the same benefit they just received. Be a smart marketer and help them share the best information. Tell people your name. If you use a hashtag, tell them what it is. Help them effectively market you to their friends. That's how this customer journey works to grow your market.

Once your customer goes through this journey and you've delivered value, your advertising job becomes very easy. Nurture the relationship with occasional communication,

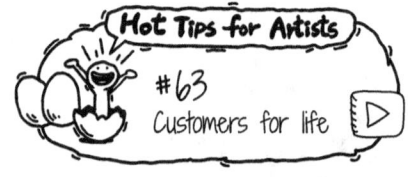

then simply let them know when your next emotional art experience is going to happen. Make sure that your existing customers and fans are aware of your next venture, your next exhibition, your next painting, your next concert, your next book. Use pull marketing. Help them become aware, help them do some research, and the cycle continues.

You can encourage customers who have completed the cycle with you to bring a friend to experience the impact of your work. Ask them to bring someone new to your world and your artwork. They will if you make it easy for them to do so. Offer them a discount. Offer them a coupon that they can send to a friend. Help them become marketers for you.

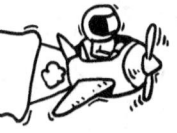

> Social media makes it easy for your fans
> to becomes marketers for you.

I encourage you to examine your social media and your online presence and clean it up. Make sure that it's easy and effortless for your customers to move to the next phase along the customer journey. If they have trouble finding you, following you, or moving to the next phase, they'll drop out before committing. They haven't yet received the direct immersive emotional impact and benefit of your work. They don't yet know its value. They've heard about it, but if it's too hard to navigate your customer journey, they will abandon the effort. Your art won't get the chance to touch them. Consider what you can do to facilitate this journey online and on social media.

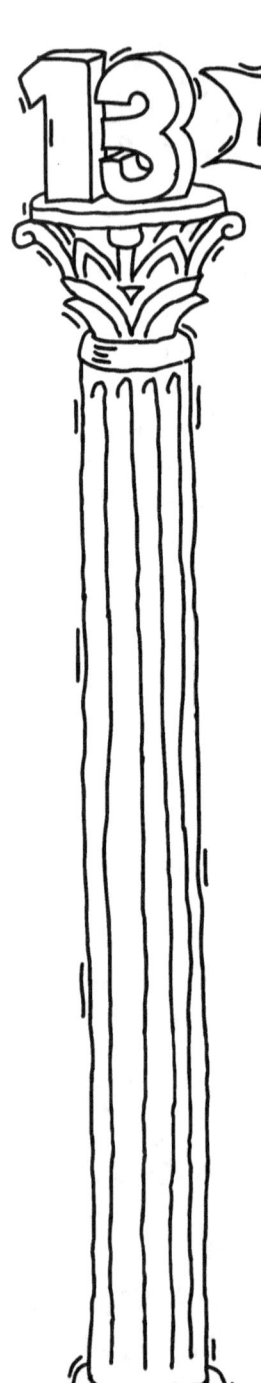

Marketing Campaigns = Audience Development

Every time you put something out into the marketplace, there's an opportunity to grow your audience and to develop a bigger market. When you develop marketing campaigns for new products or new services, you are developing your audience.

Sadly, we meet many artists have no database of customers or of ticket buyers. Rebuilding your audience every time you go to market is hard.

Think about this
The easiest sale is the second sale, the hardest sale is the first sale.

If you're going to the marketplace and trying to drum up an audience from scratch every time you produce a show, you are not building a sustainable business. Also, this strategy doesn't value your customers. It's important for you to maintain some kind of database. Start with your email list. Start to build and maintain your database using email service providers such as MailChimp or Constant Contact (there are a bunch).

You must have a database of your customers. Your job is to build a relationship with them. You can maintain that relationship through email or through posts on social media. I recommend email because it's still the best means of communicating directly with them.

I bet you spend a lot of energy working on ways to sell your art, and most of that effort results in one-off sales. You're going to be producing a lot of art. Build a relationship with your customers. You want to move your customer from being a one-off purchaser to a customer for life, a raving fan. Because they receive a benefit and your work has emotional impact, they will repeatedly buy from you. They are not going to buy every painting you produce or come to every performance, but they will market you to others who will come instead.

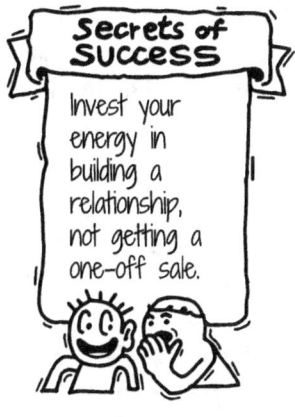

You have three opportunities to engage with your market and your customers, and each one can turn into a marketing campaign. You have an opportunity to engage with them before your art hits the marketplace. That campaign is called **'Building Anticipation.'** You have another opportunity while your art is available in the marketplace. That campaign is called **'Managing Expectations.'** And then you have an opportunity to create a third marketing campaign after your customers have experienced the art, and that's called **'Sustaining Relationships.'**

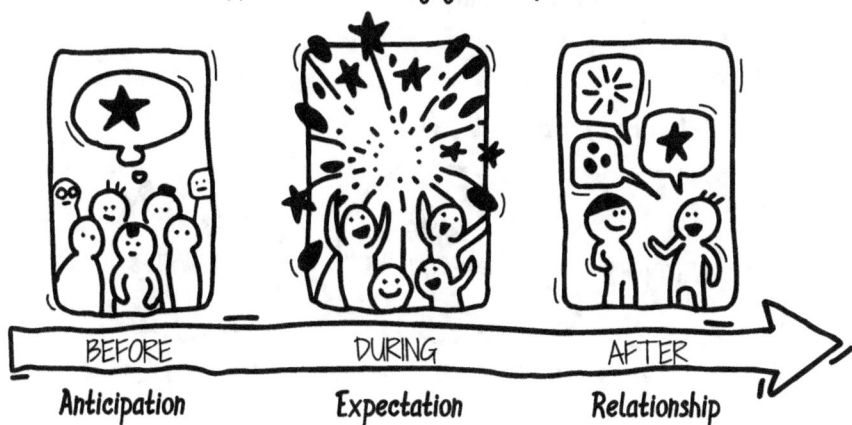

You have 3 Opportunities to engage with your customers

BEFORE — Anticipation

DURING — Expectation

AFTER — Relationship

Before: Depending on the kind of art you create, some benefits occur way before your art is actually available to be experienced. Those of you who develop community projects know that gathering the community together, and getting all those people excited about your project is one of the biggest benefits of the whole experience.

Think about your work, think about the benefits people get in anticipation of your art.

During: Some of the benefits occur **during** the direct experience of your art. Your job is to help them understand how to experience it in the best manner possible and how to receive the most benefit from it. Help them understand, and be ready for the emotional experience of your art.

After: Finally, some of the benefits happen after the experience. As they walk home, as they discuss the experience with their friends, as they think about it, as they do more research, they receive more benefits of your art after the direct experience is over.

I encourage you to do more than just an anticipation marketing campaign. In your desperation for one-off sales, you ignore what you can do to build and sustain your market. You want to nurture the customer who is going to stay with you for life. To achieve market security for you and your art, you must have more than one marketing campaign.

Here's how:

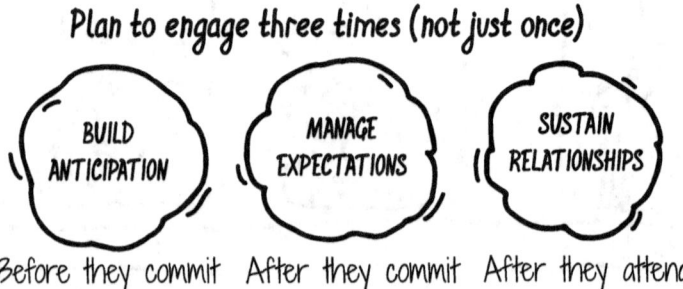

Plan to engage three times (not just once)

BUILD ANTICIPATION	MANAGE EXPECTATIONS	SUSTAIN RELATIONSHIPS
Before they commit	After they commit	After they attend

Typically, before they commit and book to attend you need to run an anticipation campaign. Let your existing market and your niche market know that your art is coming. Use pull marketing tactics. Help them begin your customer journey.

The next time you want to engage with them is after they've committed to engage with you. Approximately 48 hours before they're going to experience the art, send them an email that explains how to engage with the work. This email manages their expectations.

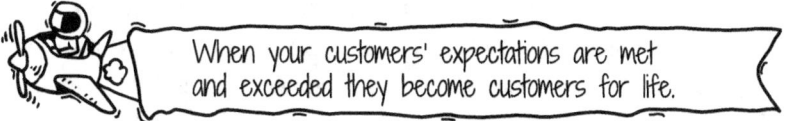

When your customers' expectations are met and exceeded they become customers for life.

Tell them what's going to happen, explain the impact that can be experienced so that they are sensitised to your art. If your art is challenging, help them. Give them examples, explain the art form, and share the back story to make the experience easier for them.

And then, you need to follow up with a third campaign to develop and **sustain relationships**. After they've experienced the art, 48 to 72 hours later, you need to send them an impact survey.

You want to ask them about their experience of your art. Ask them what they thought about during the experience, what they felt, what they think now, how they've been changed, and how the work impacted them. This dialogue is crucial to sustaining a relationship. They've just had a very cool emotional experience with you and your art. Let them tell you about it and how it affected them. Share reviews. Share how it's affected other people.

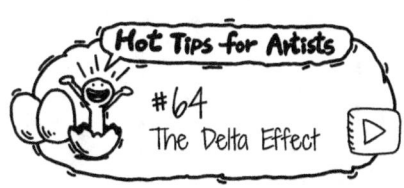

Hot Tips for Artists

#64
The Delta Effect

If you're a visual artist, after the purchase, ask your customer to send you a photo of where your work is placed in their house. Ask them to tell you what they tell other people about the artwork. Ask them for the reactions from their friends and family about the art. Ask them why they purchased your art. Build a relationship with them. If they've purchased a piece of your art, they've chosen to take a piece of your love and your energy and have it in their home.

Ask about impact after your exhibition is over. Contact the people who signed the guestbook. Remind them of what they saw. Tell them how things went for you and the gallery. Ask them how they connected personally to your art.

No matter your art form, plan to engage with your customers three times. After you've built anticipation, help them understand how to best experience your work, and then put some effort into sustaining the relationship after the sale. Once you do this, your marketing becomes progressively simpler for your repeat customer.

If there is a long gap between shows, exhibitions, or novels, you may need to remind your customers of the impact and the value of the work they last experienced. Help them reconnect to the memory of that impact. Remember, anyone who finds value in you and your art can't be kept away. All you need to do is to let them know that those benefits and that value are going to be available again soon. The one thing that makes a successful business different from an unsuccessful business is repeat customers.

Your messaging will build bigger markets and produce more customers for you when you can talk about the value, the benefit, and the impact of your art and when you can share what you do and why you do it with your niche market. It's your job to help your customers become customers for life.

Story of Success
Sara Catena

Sara Catena is a happiness catalyst. That is her brand. When people see her work, she asks them, "How does it make you feel?" Inevitably, they say, "Happy!" Even years after knowing how people will answer, she still asks. Recently, while buying her third piece of art from Sara, one woman said, "I feel happy! Your work makes me feel happy. I want to fill my house with 'happy'!" Sara's message is about happiness and connecting people to radical joy. Her market is people looking for the emotional experience of joy and happiness. (*It's a pretty big market.*)

Sara came into the Artists Transformation School after the death of her husband. Looking back, she sees that in losing her husband and allowing herself to experience the full emotions of pain and sadness, she also gained access to much bigger happiness and joy.

Her husband looked after the business side of her arts practice. After his death, Sara was forced to look after everything herself. There was a whole lot of stuff she didn't know about, and she didn't even know where to get the answers. Sara says, "I needed it in language I could relate to, and when I heard John Paul, it was a breath of fresh air. He was using language from his own experience as an artist and spiritual language that made sense to me. I knew that the Artists Transformation School would help me find the answers to thriving as a professional artist."

Sara was a practising artist, but without a marketing plan, without business knowledge, and missing a piece of her creative mojo. The experience of ATS helped Sara evolve as an artist of value. Previously, she hadn't felt that great about being an artist. She thought it was a bit of a luxury and that she wasn't contributing that much to the world. Now she feels that her contribution is crucial. "Knowing I'm making people feel happy and connecting them to that joy that is innate is incredibly valuable," she says. Sara used to think of herself and her work as separate parts. "Now I know that the whole thing is one package. Who I am in the world is my art," she confirms.

Before ATS, her marketing was haphazard. She would just post images of her paintings on social media and hope that people would buy them. "I don't do that at all any more… I spruik myself now. I share quotes that come out of me, or what I'm reading, that link back to me and my art. My branding is locked in. I don't have to ask people to 'buy my work.' Instead, I put myself out there. Those little bites of joy of who I am… I didn't know that was valuable… now I deeply know that is my value, that is who I am, it's what I paint, it's how I speak to people."

Consolidating her brand and developing her skills using value-based language have built up her markets. She offers this metaphor of her situation, "Before, I felt loose, I was a bag of apples, but only just the apples, laying on the bench. I didn't know how to gather them. I was looking for a fruit bowl to put all those apples in, to make them look pretty. I knew exactly where each one sat, and I knew what their purpose was. I needed context. I was the fruit, but I didn't have a context for any of it." Now Sara has built a strong business around her art.

The Artists Transformation School also gave Sara the structure and practice to support her business. "I do something every day, I'm clear about what my purpose is. ATS was a huge part of teaching me how to learn, and I've kept learning ever since. I'm constantly learning new things that fit into my practice and my business. I'm tackling my learning head on. I love my morning practice, and the mother list. Both have evolved. I work this stuff every day... do my hard stuff first. I also do something every day that will take me toward where I want to go... I also do affirmations every day and have a vision book I look at every day. ATS has given me the tools to know that I can thrive and achieve the things I want to."

Sara has grown her market while diversifying her income. She continues to exhibit her work and sell it. She is also making money from her creativity, not just her art. She's mentoring other artists, she's working online with a school in Uruguay and, most recently, with a teacher and school in Bahrain, where she is helping them monetise their creative curriculum online.

"Before, I thought I was a just painter... now the idea of me as an artist is so much more. There is so much I can do with who I am and with my work." Sara has chosen four words for the year: **FOCUS, EXPANSION, GREATNESS, and CONTRIBUTION.** On the contribution front, she is the Art Ambassador for a health foundation and is working with two major hospitals to spread happiness and joy through art. "Those ideas and opportunities have come because I have an open mind to multiple streams... I don't see myself the way I did before."

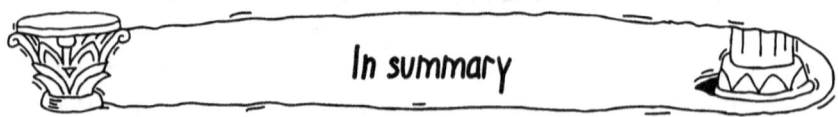

In summary

This section on marketing and message could be enormous. There's a lot to learn about building your market and communicating your message. I've tried to give you some very essential and practical tips to help make this pillar strong enough to support your sustainable arts business.

Many artists waste a lot of time and money on advertising and marketing because they aren't doing it effectively. Your job is to find the people who will love you and your art the most. Let them know that you are the source of the benefits they're looking for. Spend 30% of your time sharing your work with them.

Building a relationship with your customer is the key to growing your market. In the past, you just put the art out there. You didn't understand the needs of the broker who gave you the opportunity to present your work. You ignored the customer. You can't possibly know all the people sitting in those seats facing the stage. You don't know all the people coming through the gallery, looking at your work, and being excited by it. Often, the brokers of those experiences have kept you distanced from your customer. But with social media and e-marketing, you can establish a relationship with them. Your customer will reach out to you if you help them do so. If they can find you, they can get more value from your art. And if you reach out to them and build a relationship of value, they will stay with you.

Don't move on to the next chapter without taking some action in the next 48 hours.

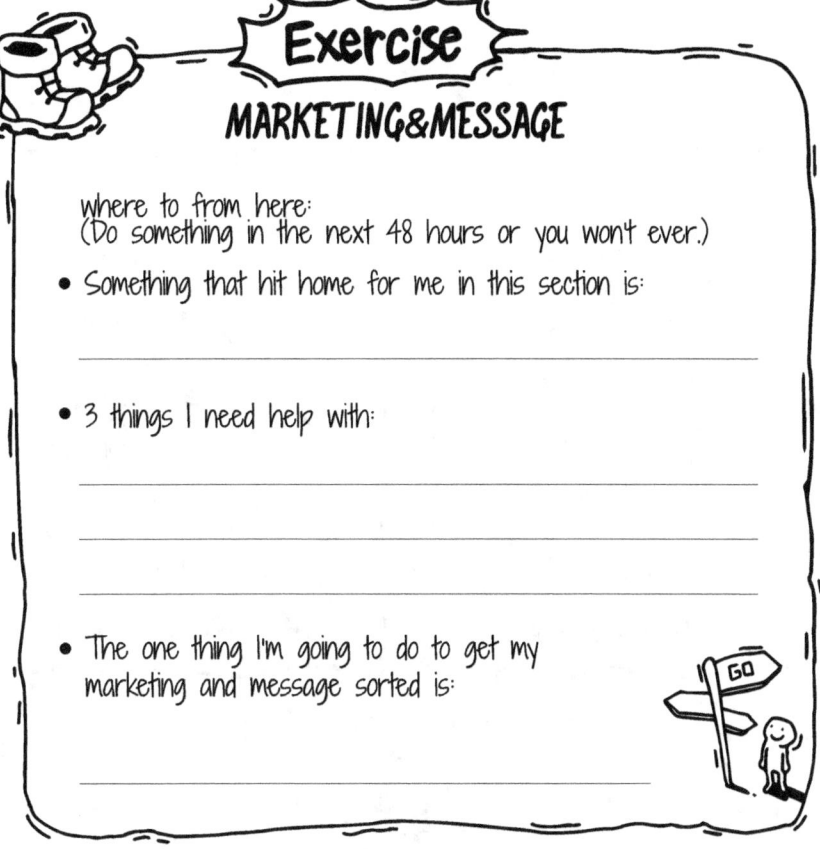

Exercise

MARKETING&MESSAGE

where to from here:
(Do something in the next 48 hours or you won't ever.)

- Something that hit home for me in this section is:

  _____

- 3 things I need help with:

  _____

  _____

  _____

- The one thing I'm going to do to get my marketing and message sorted is:

  _____

Artists before you have identified the top six things from this section as worthy of their focus:

1. Know the need I meet.

2. Share, don't sell.

3. Network more.

4. Use value-based language.

5. Build a customer avatar.

6. Use all three opportunities to engage with my customers.

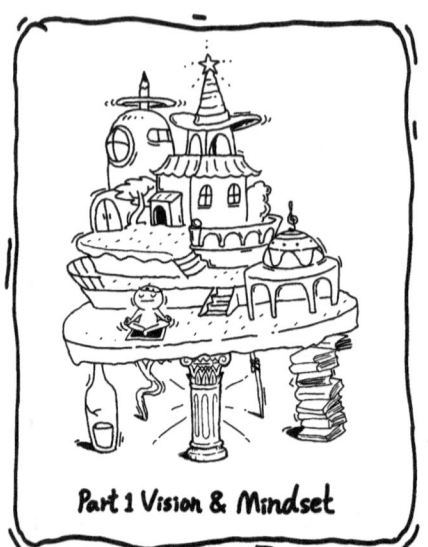

Part 1 Vision & Mindset

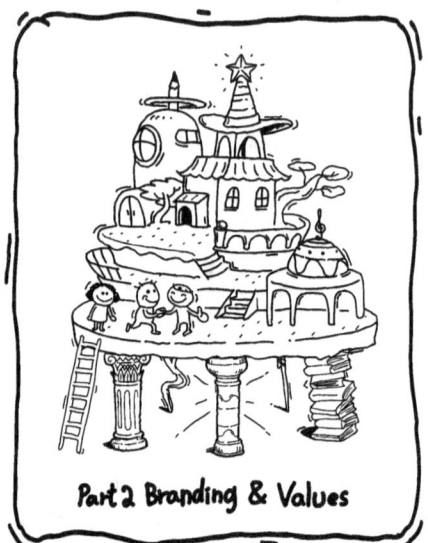

Part 2 Branding & Values

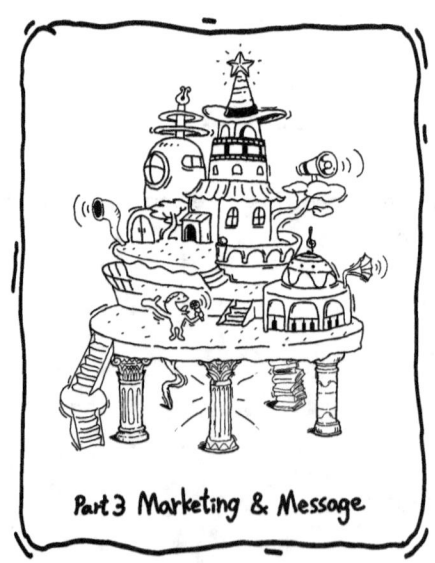

Part 3 Marketing & Message

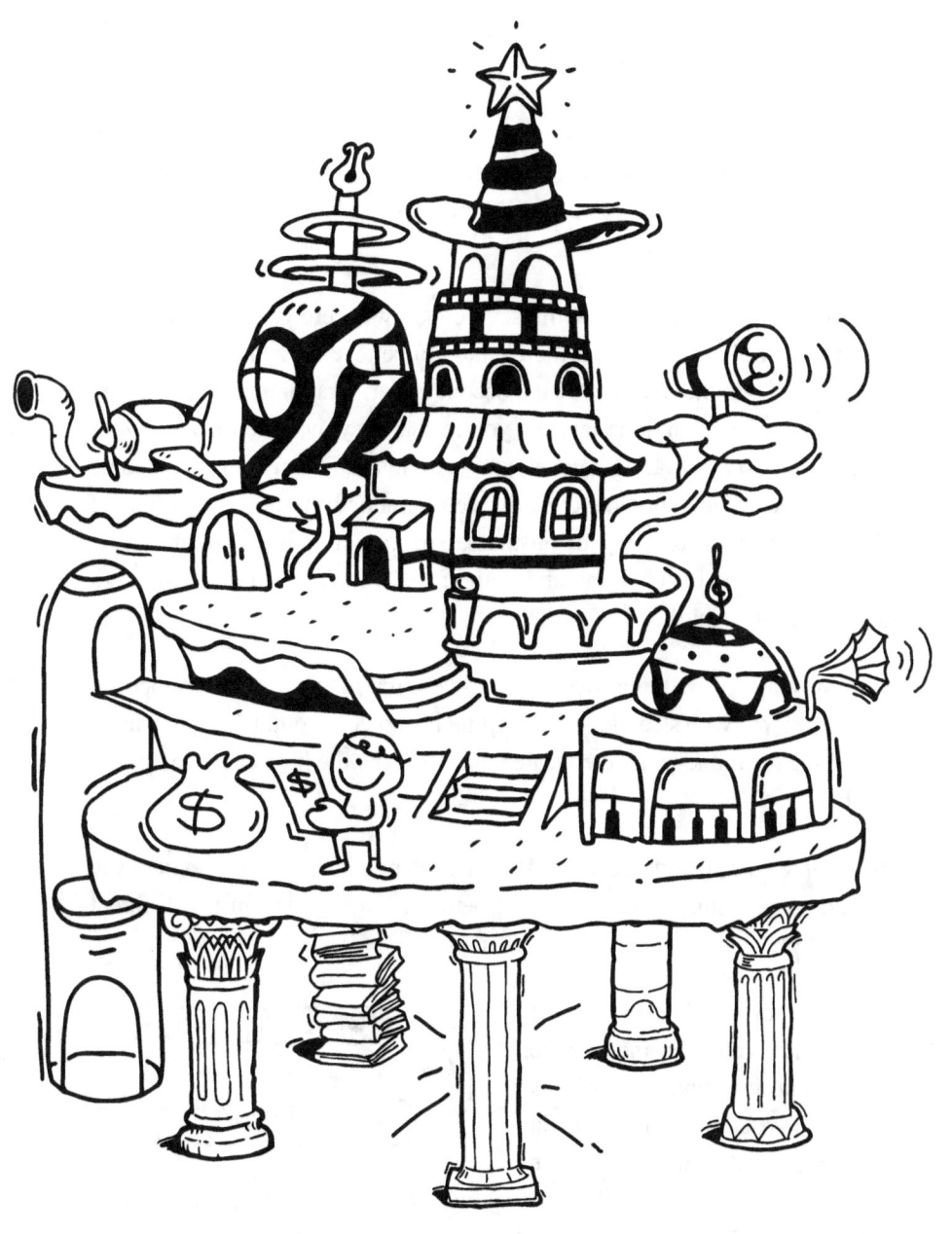

Part 4 Money & Finance

In this section, you're going to manage your money and get comfortable seeing your art from the numbers.

Let's check on your journey towards creating your own sustainable small business. You've erected the first three fundamental pillars. With these three pillars in place, you now have a solid and sustainable foundation for your business.

With the first pillar, Vision & Mindset, you know where you're headed, you know how you're going to get there, and you believe that you will succeed. Added to this is the strength of the second pillar, Branding & Values. You have an awesome brand in play, and you're sharing your likeability and your enthusiasm. You're valuing yourself and your time, and you know that people are attracted to your brand. Recently, you've added the powerful pillar of Marketing & Message to your business. You can effectively communicate the value and the benefits you and your art deliver, and you have begun to grow your niche market.

The advantage of building these three pillars first is that you now support a viable business with steady money coming in and going out. It's time to learn to manage the money and to educate yourself about the financial side of your arts business.

Being able to see your business in terms of numbers is just another way of describing your business. It's not better or worse—it's just a different perspective.

Some people will be able to understand your business when you explain it in numbers. You can say, "I have a small business that turns over $200,000 a year." They

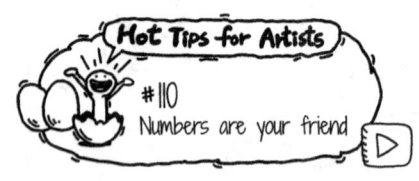

Hot Tips for Artists
#110
Numbers are your friend

understand the kind of small business you have because they know what that figure means. Similarly, some people will understand where you're trying to go when you explain your business goals in numbers. When talking about marketing, you could say, "I want to double my database to 5,000 people." The way you describe your business is how people understand your business. You could also say to someone, "I currently bring in $100,000. Next year

I'd like to have earned $150,000." It's just a different way for people to understand your goals. The language of numbers is an easy way for you to talk about and manage your business.

In this section, let's look at managing your money, financial literacy, and making more money. I want to kick off this section with a little exercise.

Exercise

MY FINANCIAL HEALTH

$ _____ per year is what I need.

$ _____ per year is what I earn.

I earn $ _____ from my art and creativity.

I earn $ _____ from another source.

My financial goal for this year is $ _____ .

Pause and fill in this little chart.

✓ *Write down the amount of money you need per year – not the number you want, but the number you need. Do you know what that number is?*

✓ *Then, write down the total amount per year you currently earn from all sources.*

✓ *Then, get inside that number and identify what you earn from your art and your creativity.*

The money that you earn in any given year might come from a variety of sources. Some of those sources of income might not be your arts practice. I would like you to get a handle on the amount of money you earn from your creativity and your art. If you want this business to become the thing you do fulltime, without also maintaining some other part-time job, then it's important to know the gap between your total income and how much you earn from your creative activity.

✓ *Then, write a number in the next line, "I earned X from another source."*

You need to see those two numbers side by side, because that establishes a goal and sends a message to your subconscious to reach a target.

✓ *Finally, create your financial goal for this year.*

Be realistic, but make it a stretch. Consider what you need, where you want to go, and how much time and energy and focus you can devote to your arts business in the year.

Setting a financial goal is perhaps one of the most important things you will learn to do in this section. Setting a financial goal acts like magic for artists, because you are such a fabulous manifestor of your visions. In the first section, we talked about mindset. You're an incredible entrepreneur. You can create something that never existed before. You can conquer obstacles. You can gather the resources you need. When you have a goal and a target to hit, chances are that you'll hit it. Have a financial goal for this year.

Being able to talk about your numbers is being in business. If you're a hobbyist, you never need to talk about the numbers, because you're financing the hobby. Your hobby provides benefits and good feelings, so you're happy to fund it. It's not a business. It becomes a business when you have customers, when you have multiple products that you put out in the marketplace.

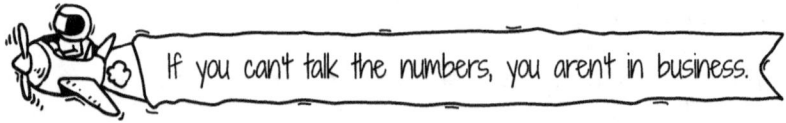

If you can't talk the numbers, you aren't in business.

Many artists come to us and ask, "Will this work?" There's no easy answer to that. It comes down to whether the business idea, the art, the art product, or the service is viable. If you are trying to figure out if your idea is viable, the only two measures that matter are:

1. **Is there a market for it?**

2. **Do you want to do it for the long haul?**

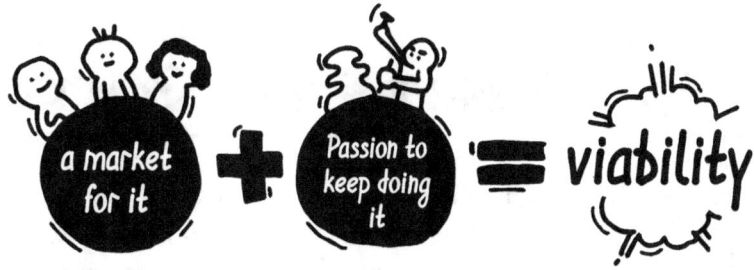

The first test, when you're introducing a new product or a new service into a market, is to find out whether there is actually a need for it.

I once worked with a woodcarver who was making carvings that he thought the market would buy. Unfortunately, they weren't selling. When he started asking around, he learned that there was no need for those particular types of carvings in his immediate geographic market. The same product or a similar product was available from overseas at one quarter of the price he needed to charge. Jim quickly realised that there was no market for the product he could create. So, he re-examined his values and what was important to him. He looked at what he loved to carve and realised that he could carve something unique and different. And when he talked to people about the product that was more aligned to his values, he found that there was a market for that. It's important to establish if there's a market for your art product or service. If there is, the next question is, are you motivated enough to keep creating it? Do you enjoy doing it? Will you stay with it for the long haul?

This section helps you wrap your mind and your heart around the money, the finance, and the numbers that are part of your arts business.

14 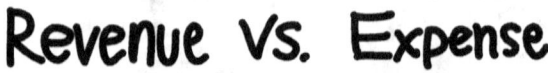 Revenue Vs. Expense

Managing the finances of your business comes down to managing two things: revenue and expenses. Revenue is the money coming in. Expenses are the money going out. The goal of your small business is to increase revenue and reduce expenses.

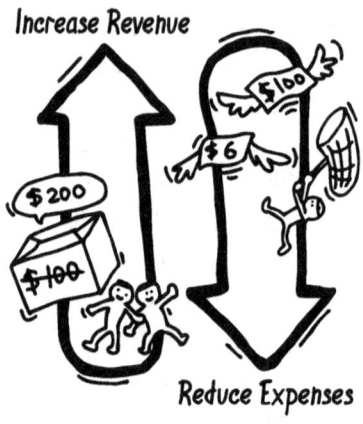

Increase Revenue

Reduce Expenses

What can you do to increase your revenue? With every month, every product, every concert, every show? Ask yourself, "What can I do to increase my revenue?" Can you raise your price? Almost 90% of the time, the answer is YES! Once you understand the impact and the value that you deliver, chances are that you can raise your price. Because you're in the emotion business, the price for your cool, awesome emotional experience is quite elastic. There aren't many places people can go to get a similar experience. Once they understand the impact, the value, and the benefits that you deliver, if they have the money, the desire, and most importantly, if they have the need, they will pay the price you ask.

Another way you can increase revenue is to increase the number of customers. In the performing arts, an incredible amount of effort is put into creating a show for one short run of a couple of weeks, and then the show gets shelved. If the show did well at the first venue, figure out how to remount that show at a larger venue. Can you take that show on tour? Can you find more people who would like to see it? You can increase your revenue by finding more customers.

If you're in the visual arts, one of your challenges is recouping the cost of making the original. Originals need to fetch a high price, but there is more than one person who will be moved by that image. You can provide that image to multiple customers by making Giclée prints or creating other products with the same design. In what ways can you give the same product to more customers?

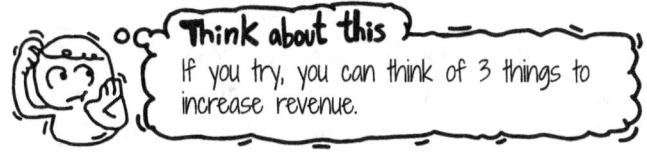

The other thing that you want is to see if there's any way to reduce expenses. Can you cut costs? After creating the first version, are there things that you know you won't need when recreating the work? Are there things you do repeatedly that you can automate? It's expensive to spend your time repeating steps when they could be automated. Are there things you could do that would reduce the amount of raw material you waste to cut costs?

Arts businesses can be very labour-intensive. Now that you value you and your time, stop doing all of the things and focus on doing the most important things. There are lots of cool things that can happen for your arts business by taking on apprentices, interns, or students. This gives you a supply of cheaper labour, while these people develop their practice, learn from a master, and get an opportunity to see how it's done.

The three simplest ways to manage your finances are as follows:

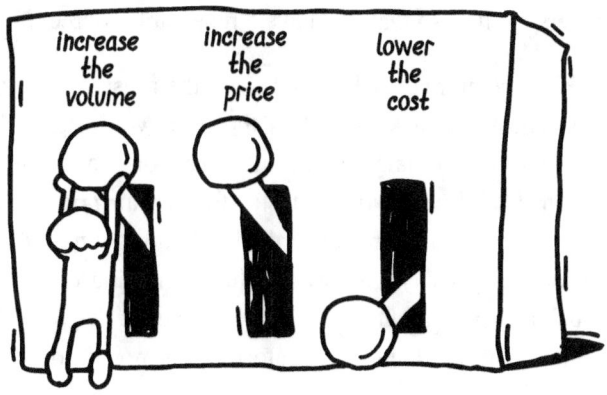

These are the three levers you can play with in managing your arts business. Can you make more of this? Can you replicate this? Can you increase the price? And what can you do to reduce the costs?

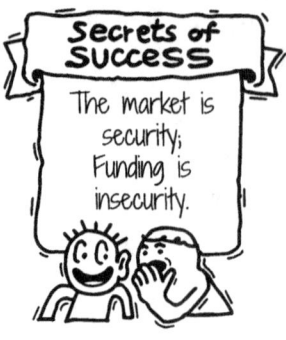

Secrets of Success

The market is security; Funding is insecurity.

When you find a market for your product and that market values your contribution as an artist, and you help your market understand the impact of your art, you build a secure market. That is secure funding. That is secure money coming in. It is recurring funding, because all you have to do is to continue to create the art and let your market know that you're producing more of the thing they value.

Grant funding is NOT security for your small business. Getting that funding once is no guarantee that you will get it again. On the other hand, knowing that you made a customer happy is a guarantee that that customer will come back when they have that need again. Of all the things that you can do to increase revenue, focusing on sales is the most important—not funding, but sales. Get more sales.

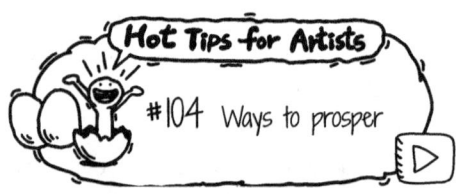

Hot Tips for Artists

#104 Ways to prosper

In the last section, we touched on the concept of renewable revenue. You don't want to keep chasing one-off sales. You want to build relationships that create customers for life, so that you have a renewable source of revenue.

OK, let's look at this more closely. If sales are the most important thing for your business, you must make sure that the price you're getting for your product or your service is fair. Figure out what you are worth. Is there a standard in your discipline or your industry for the fair price of your time? Some unions have set minimum standards. It's important that you know the industry standard for your type of work. The other thing necessary for fair exchange is being honest about the real time it takes to deliver your product or service. Often, the products we create require months of work, so it's difficult for us to determine the amount of time that's gone into the creation of a particular art piece. But it's important to figure this out, because you cannot manage what you cannot measure.

Regardless of whether it takes three months or three hours to create your art, it's important to be able to figure out the time required. If you were to examine that three-month period and count the actual hours you spent on the work, you could probably come up with a number. Do that. You want to know that the product or service you create generates enough revenue to make it worth the investment of your time.

You can see that it's important to be able to come to terms with numbers. Discover the numbers. Learn to talk about the numbers. If you're going to manage your business, you need to be able to find ways of increasing revenue and reducing expenses. You need to be making the income you need from your sales.

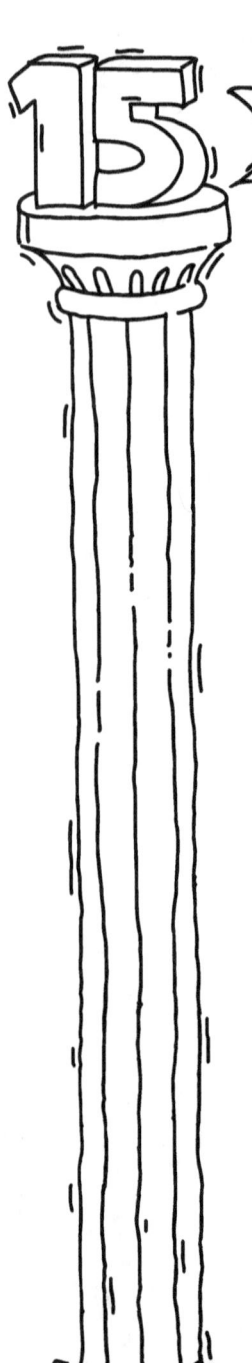

Pricing Your Product or Service

We've worked with many artists who have no idea where to begin pricing their work. What holds their business back from succeeding is that they don't accurately price their art.

Some are caught between giving their art away to people who love and value it and feel its impact, and selling it to people who love it, value it and feel the impact. It's important for you to understand what's involved in pricing your art. Here's a very simple formula that helps you understand the principles of pricing your work so that your work generates the income you need.

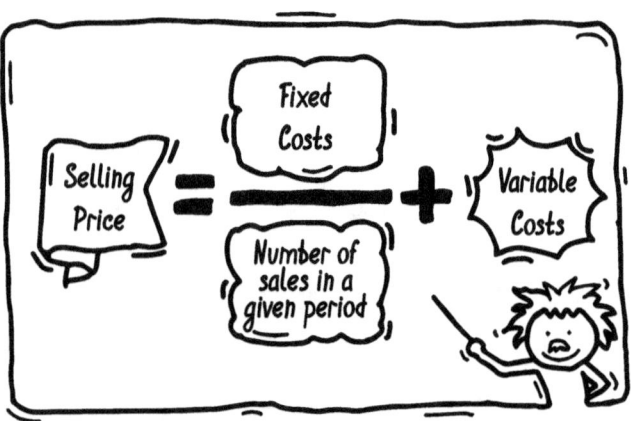

$$\text{Selling Price} = \frac{\text{Fixed Costs}}{\text{Number of sales in a given period}} + \text{Variable Costs}$$

In Chapter 17, we will look at your fixed costs more closely. But for now, understand that being in business means that you have fixed costs that don't change whether you produce any art or not. Your website must be hosted and maintained. Your mobile phone bill must be paid regardless of what you create. There is petrol for your car. There is rent for your studio. There is public liability insurance. These are some of the fixed costs every artist has.

It's time to wrap your brain around your fixed costs—what it costs just to be operating your artistic practice as a business. Take your fixed costs and divide it by the number of sales in a given period.

When you know your fixed costs for a year, you can figure out how many products or services you need to sell in a year. This number important to the part of you that is the CEO and director of finance. Every time you produce a product or a service, it must cover a portion of your fixed costs.

In addition to fixed costs, you have variable costs. Those are the costs that can vary depending on the size, scope, or scale of the artistic product or service that you create. You can determine your lowest selling price by adding these two.

This isn't a hard and fast formula. It doesn't work for every artist and every art product or service. But it covers a fundamental principle of pricing your work. Many artists we work with have not grasped the concept that every product or service they create needs to contribute towards the fixed costs of running the business and has also to cover the variable costs directly associated with the creation of the product or service.

Once you understand the principle of fixed and variable costs, you're able to look at the numbers and manage them. Don't be alarmed when you see the result of this formula and realise that the price you need to charge for your art is astronomically greater than you think the market will pay. That's all right. Go back and examine what you can do to reduce the costs, increase the volume, or increase the price. Simply being aware of this number sets you off on the right journey towards understanding the amount of money you need to charge if you're going to cover all your costs over a year, over a month, over six months, or whatever period of time you want.

Figure out what price your market will pay. Maybe you need to decide that you're not going to produce a particular art form very often because it's price is too high. Maybe at this stage in your business it isn't realistic to demand that price. Or you might decide that it's okay to produce this kind of expensive work because you can leverage it. Or you decide to invest this time and money for the next three years to establish your brand.

It's your business. It's your decision. Maybe you will decide that once a year, you're going to invest in a very large, expensive, and time-consuming art project or service to establish yourself as 'Best in Class' in the market. You're going to grow your market by establishing yourself as a leader in your art form. That's OK, it's your business. You can choose to invest in creating something that's going to have a positive impact on the business that does not necessarily have a positive financial impact. Just be aware of this choice. Create ways to generate the money you need to cover your fixed costs and the investment in this one big bold thing.

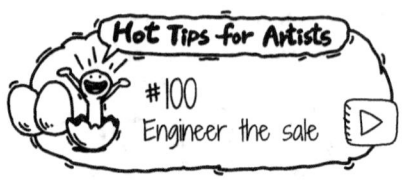

When looking at your market's willingness to pay, one of the questions you need to ask is, "Are there similar things to this in the market?" If there are similar things, do some research, see what price they charge. See how you are different. Similarly, imagine their customer avatar. Your market might be more willing to pay, because you've done really well at the Marketing and Message stage, and you have successfully communicated the value, the benefits, and the impact of your work, so you're in a much more flexible position for pricing.

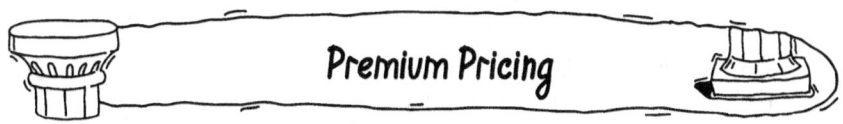

Premium Pricing

If this is the only chance people have to experience your amazing art, you can charge more. That's the principle of **premium pricing**. When establishing the price for your art, think about premium pricing. Is there some additional value you can include that makes the formula: Sale = ART + X? Is there a provision for VIP access? "This is the normal price, but if you want special access to behind the scenes, if you want a closer table, if you want to attend the rehearsal, if you want to get a backstage tour, if you want to come and visit the studio, there is a premium price." There can be various things you add to create premium pricing without having to create more product.

We've taught a lot of visual artists to offer premium pricing for framing, installing, and lighting their artwork. Nobody understands better than you the play of light on your art or how far away people need to be from it for the optimal experience. You can charge for coming and installing the art in your customer's house.

Another premium pricing opportunity is when there is a limited supply of your product. If this is the only concert, if this is the only time you're going to perform in this region, if this only happens for one night, you can increase your price. If there is a limited supply, customers understand that and pay more. Similarly, in the visual arts, if this product is the original, it is unique and people understand that it is more expensive. When you do a print run of forty-five pieces, and someone knows that they're purchasing number 41, they know that there are only four left. You can increase the price due to the limited supply. Think about premium pricing for your work. You're in the arts business. You don't generate thousands of experiences. You generate a small number of very intimate experiences.

Also think about how you exceed expectations. Once you've set your price and delivered the art, take a moment and reflect on how you exceeded the customer's expectations. Knowing this gives you pricing leverage. Your market might have an expectation that they simply buy a work of art, and that's it—they'll have no further encounter with the artist. But once you start exceeding their expectations and you build a relationship, you can help them see more value in the price you charge. Do you share the story behind the art? Do you take a photo with you and the purchaser and the art and post it on social media? Do you stay in touch after the sale? For many of, us exceeding expectations is just the way we do business.

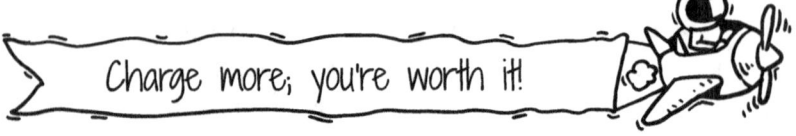

Charge more; you're worth it!

Help your customers appreciate the value you deliver. Help yourself understand, measure, and manage the numbers to make sure that the pricing for your product or service is desirable, reasonable, acceptable, and achievable.

If you invite your fans to support your vision, to support your idea, to help you realise some cool thing, they will take up your invitation because they like you. They see the value in you as an artist. They're willing to support your project and pay your price because they want you to succeed. They want to support your vision.

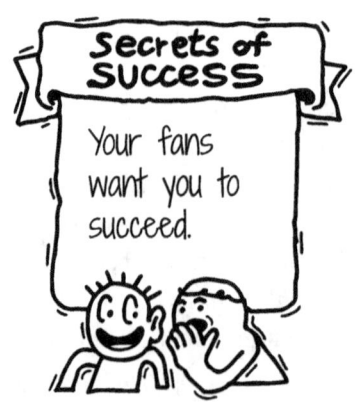

Secrets of Success

Your fans want you to succeed.

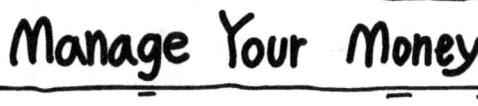

Manage Your Money

In this chapter, I want to introduce you to some practical tools to help you get better at managing your money. I know that when you set your mind to it, you can learn whatever you need to learn. I also know that in your arts career you have learned way more complex things than managing an Excel spreadsheet.

Managing your money is just a new skill like any other. Being able to track and measure your money is just a skill that you don't yet have. Well, just learn it. Get some help if you need to. You're only going to need short-term help. It's not rocket science to learn how Excel helps you to set up a simple system of tracking and entering your data and adding up a column of numbers. Creating an Excel spreadsheet is just a new skill to learn.

In running your arts business, you must be aware of your finances. You must be able to look at what it has cost you to be an artist this month and figure out what it will cost you next month. You must be able to compare the money that you

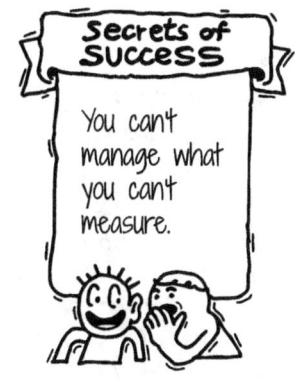

Secrets of Success

You can't manage what you can't measure.

spent with the money that you earned. You must be able to understand a budget and build a budget. This is your new learning curve as an artist in business. Managing your money uses skills in a part of your brain that may be underdeveloped. Well suck it up, get over it, and start working out. The first step is financial tracking.

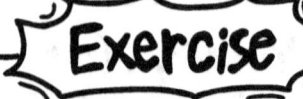

Exercise

Financial Tracking

For the next 3 months track every bit of money going out and every bit coming in.

Step 1. Track your spending by keeping an expense diary.

Step 2. At the end of the month tally your figures.

Step 3. Account for items paid quarterly or yearly.

Step 4. Record all your income for the month

Step 5 Analyze the figures

For the next three months, I want you to track every bit of money going out and every bit of money coming in. Be ruthless and voraciously curious. It will be hard for the first month and way easier by the third. Here are five steps to start measuring your finances.

Step 1. Track your spending by keeping an expense diary. *Go get a little notebook, build a spreadsheet, or download an app. Carry it with you everywhere you go to keep track of everything you spend. Try and make the distinction between personal expenses and expenses for your business. You're going to be interested in both, because your lifestyle includes your arts practice.*

Step 2. At the end of the month, tally these figures. *Transfer all your purchases to another document. Generate a spreadsheet, or just make a list. At the end of the month, I want you to transfer all the purchases to one document and tally them up.*

Step 3. Account for items that you pay for quarterly or yearly. *Things like hosting your domain name is a yearly expense. You need to divide that by 12 and add it to each month's expenses. Some things you pay quarterly, for example, your gas bill or your electric bill. You're going to allocate those expenses to each month, so you need to divide them by 3 and add the appropriate amount to each month.*

Step 4. Record all your income for the month. *Make a record of all the money coming in and where it came from.*

Step 5. Analyse the figures. *Just look at the month. How much did you spend? What did you spend it on? How much money came in? Where did it come from? And then I want you to take a moment and actually write down any observations and thoughts you have. Don't just look at this data and have emotional reactions. Write down what you observe. Write down what you've learned. Note down some things that you need to consider as future expenses or as future income. At the end of this month, you may have spent a lot, because you are in the 'creation phase'. So, make a note that says, "The money that I spent this month is to create the work that's going to go on exhibition and on sale next month." That helps you understand how to manage the money you're starting to measure.*

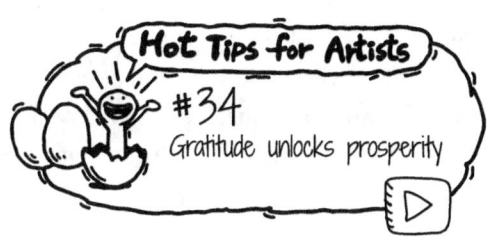

Hot Tips for Artists
#34
Gratitude unlocks prosperity

Record keeping

Keep it simple. Your record-keeping just needs to be writing down a note of money coming in and money going out. At the end of the year, once you know what it all looks like, talk to an arts accountant. It's never too early to talk to an arts accountant. Your arts accountant will be an incredible support and ally for you in building and running your business.

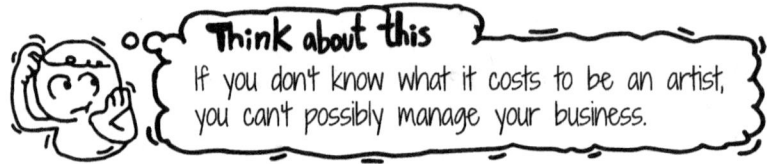

Think about this
If you don't know what it costs to be an artist, you can't possibly manage your business.

Make sure that you're clear about expenses that are business related as opposed to personal. Once you've gotten your financial tracking down, just continue to be a good record-keeper. It's a new skill. You have to do it regularly. You're going to start collecting and keeping every receipt to make the decision whether this is personal or business and then making a record of it. Once you start keeping records, you can start to manage your money. Just through this simple act of record-keeping, you're going to discover amazing things. You're going to discover, for example, that over the year, you spent $2,200 on coffee. Could you reduce that expense? How much art could you create with that money? What cool new project could you embark on? Where could you make a better investment of that $2,200?

Story of Success

Ian Mortimer Longyard Sideshow

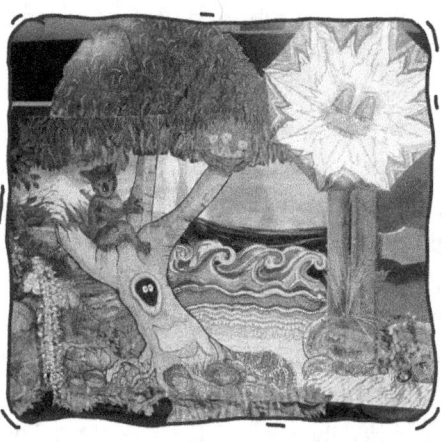

When we first met Mort, the creator and visionary behind Longyard Sideshow, he was making a modest living for himself and a small team of actors. Mort was a storyteller, writer and builder.

His major creation was a giant touring children's pop-up book that recounted the aboriginal tale of Tiddalik the Frog. After four years of touring, he had little to show for his efforts. He came into the incubator to learn business skills and to turn his touring show into a business that would make a profit and enable him to create something else.

Mort's pillar of Money & Finance was too weak to sustain the awesome creative projects he was capable of. We showed him how to manage his money and taught him the financial skills every artist needs to have in order to make a profit from touring. He was able to raise the performance fee, reduce expenses, and offer the premium pricing value add-on of workshops, training in storytelling, puppetry and environmental land care.

We helped him step by step to learn and follow the best practice industry standard policies and procedures for costing, quoting, and contracting his performances. Over seven months, he shifted paradigms from starving artist to capable entrepreneur. He developed financial literacy, basic accounting skills, executive management thinking, supervisory skills, and negotiation skills. He learned to budget and monitor his finances, as well as contract and manage actors.

Mort's niche was primary schools interested in aboriginal studies and the environment. He partnered with foundations and government bodies who sponsored tours, and he was able to 'wholesale' entire months of touring. He learned the 'business side' of his profession, built three touring companies, and ran each at a profit. This resulted in him being able to develop a business prospectus and gather sufficient financial data to license the production to a third party, who eventually toured the show independently and paid him a 20% royalty.

Sadly, Mort passed away unexpectedly. But at the end, he was using his business skills to move into project management and create commissioned kinetic sculptures. Mort was a much sought-after creator of content-driven edu-tainment for museums. His customers valued the fact that he could manage his finances.

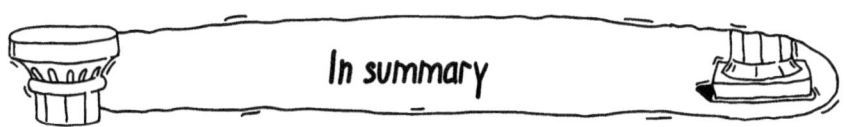

In summary

It's not okay for you to turn your head away from the money and the numbers. If you can't talk numbers, you aren't in business. If you CAN talk numbers, you will be surprised how many things will magically autocorrect. Once you begin to see your success in financial terms, you begin to feel greater ease, and your subconscious mind goes to work to find you more of that feeling. On the other hand, if you're not able to feel and talk about your financial success, your subconscious is stuck with the impression that anxiety about finances is normal and must be what you want, so it aims directs you toward that instead.

It's important to work on building a good, strong fourth pillar of money and finance so that you can manage your business for growth. You will be a genuine artist in a successful and sustainable business when you can talk numbers and manage your money.

Don't move on to the next chapter without taking some action in the next 48 hours.

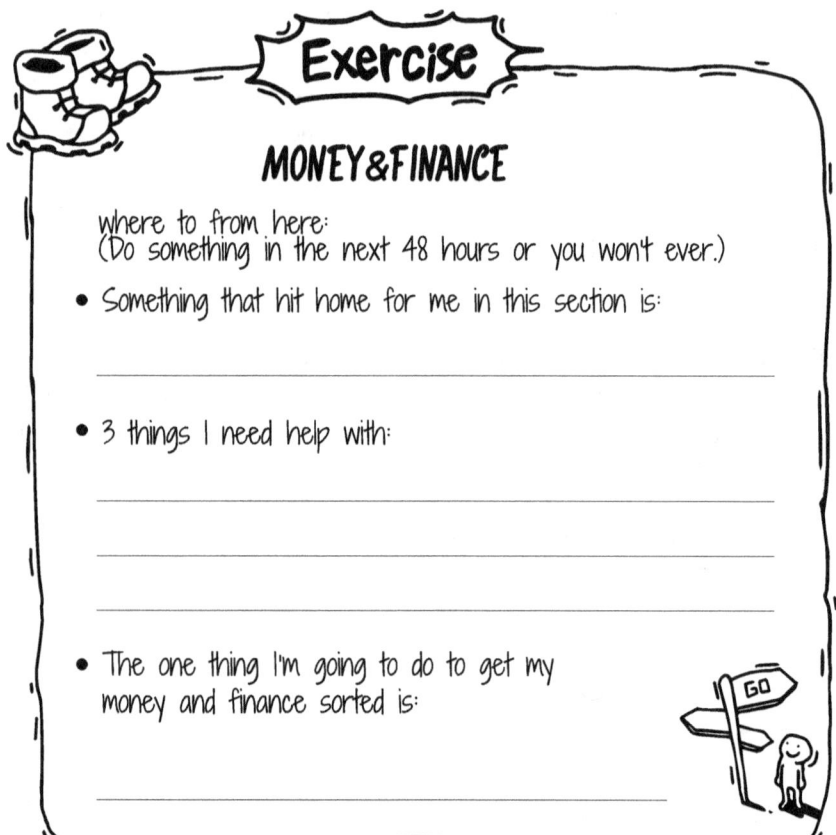

Exercise

MONEY&FINANCE

where to from here:
(Do something in the next 48 hours or you won't ever.)

- Something that hit home for me in this section is:

_____

- 3 things I need help with:

_____

_____

_____

- The one thing I'm going to do to get my money and finance sorted is:

_____

Artists before you have identified these top six things from this section as worthy of their focus.

1. Start managing my money

2. Charge what I'm worth

3. Add premium pricing

4. Describe my business in numbers

5. Increase my revenue / reduce my expenses

6. Find an arts accountant

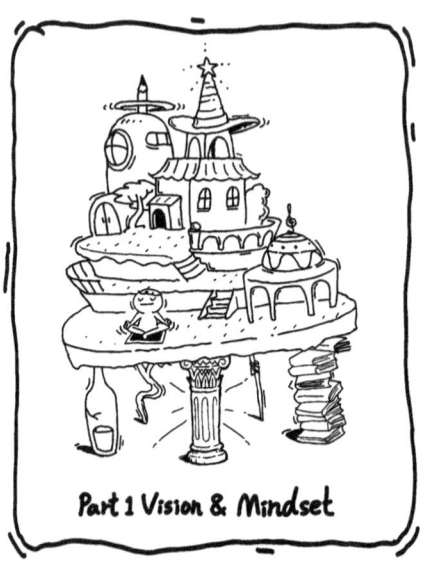

Part 1 Vision & Mindset

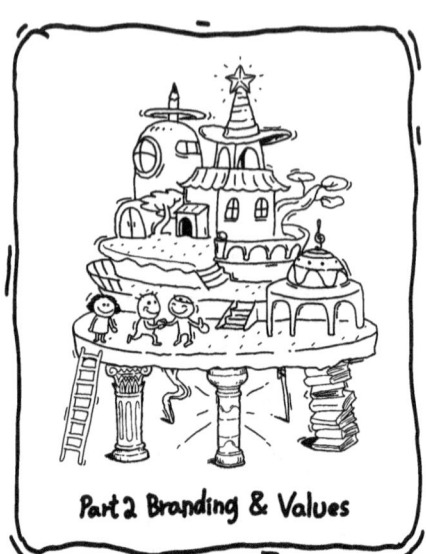

Part 2 Branding & Values

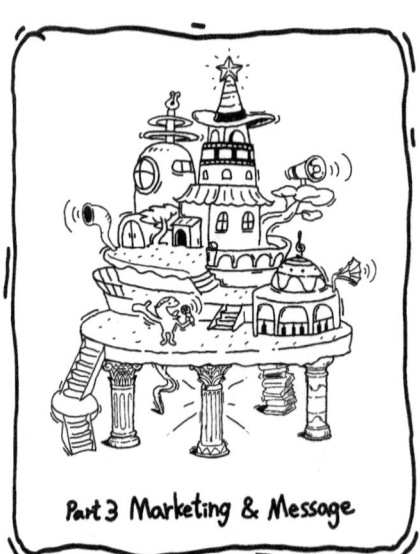

Part 3 Marketing & Message

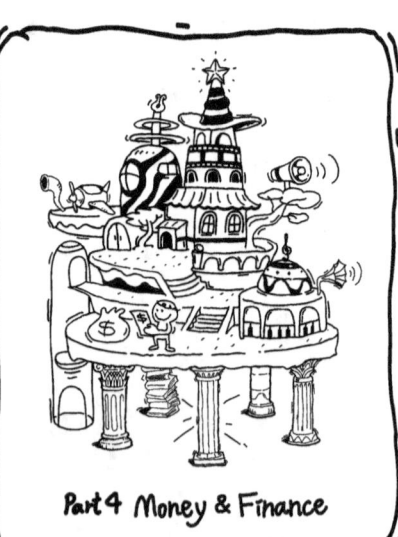

Part 4 Money & Finance

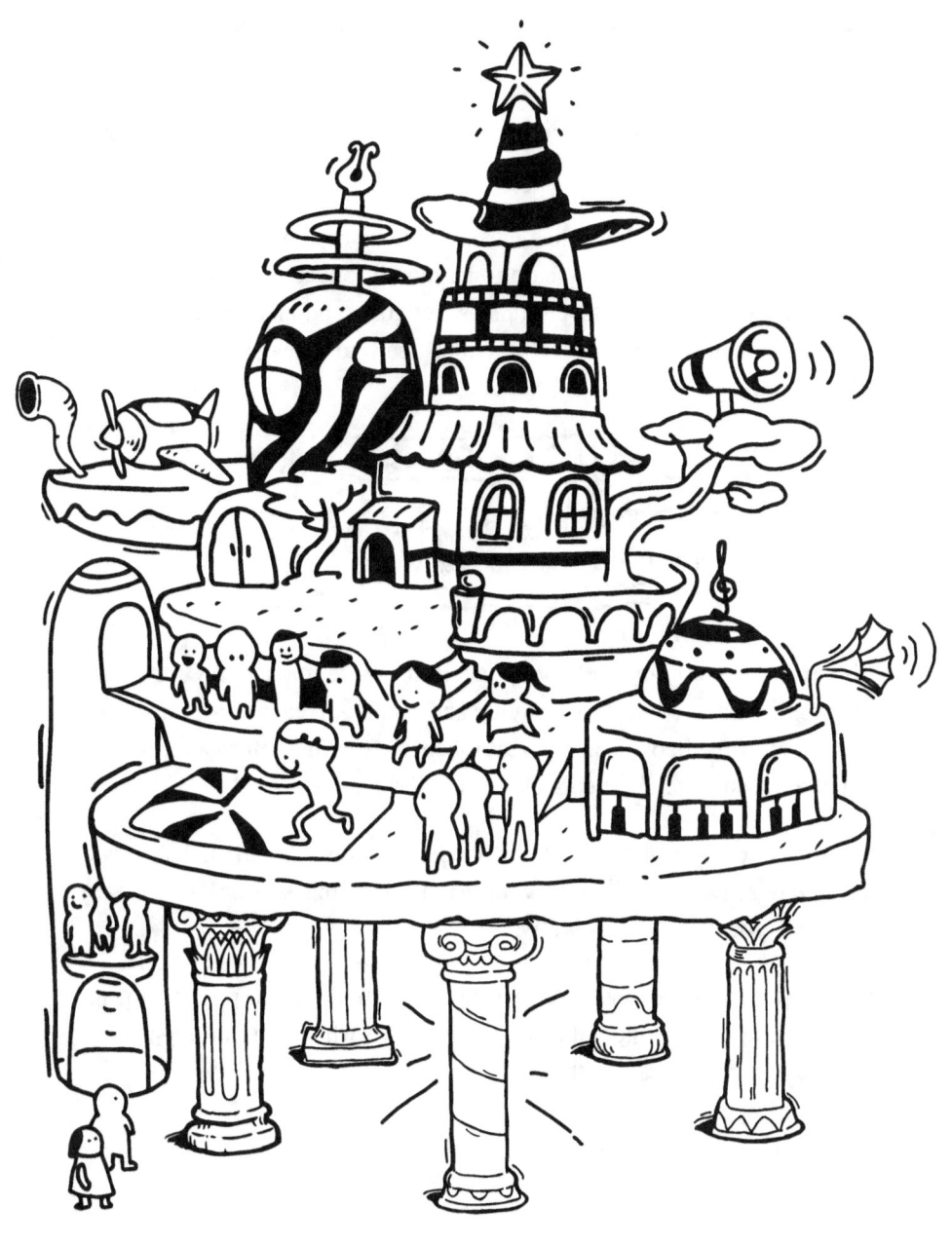

Part 5 Planning & Productivity

This section is about growing your business and managing your growth so that you don't burn out.

This fifth and final pillar is necessary now that you have a viable business with lots of customers.

You're getting busier. More sales means more work and more demands on your time. Now is the time to learn to be more productive in order to grow your business. It's time to develop plans, set goals and measure progress. It is also the time to make course corrections, learn to manage your time, and build a team.

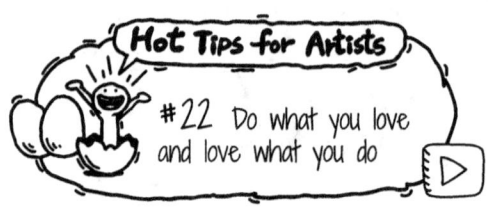

This section is not going to be very useful if you're not actually running a business. If your arts business is not up and running, feel free to skim across this section of the book. You can really benefit from the information in this section only when you immediately deploy it as you learn.

To get the most out of this section, honour the way that artists learn, and that's Learn & Do. As you make your way through this section, if you learn something, you need to do it NOW.

I want to start with another exercise using your intuition. You're going to talk to all those awesome internal advisors you have who want you to succeed and need to communicate with you.

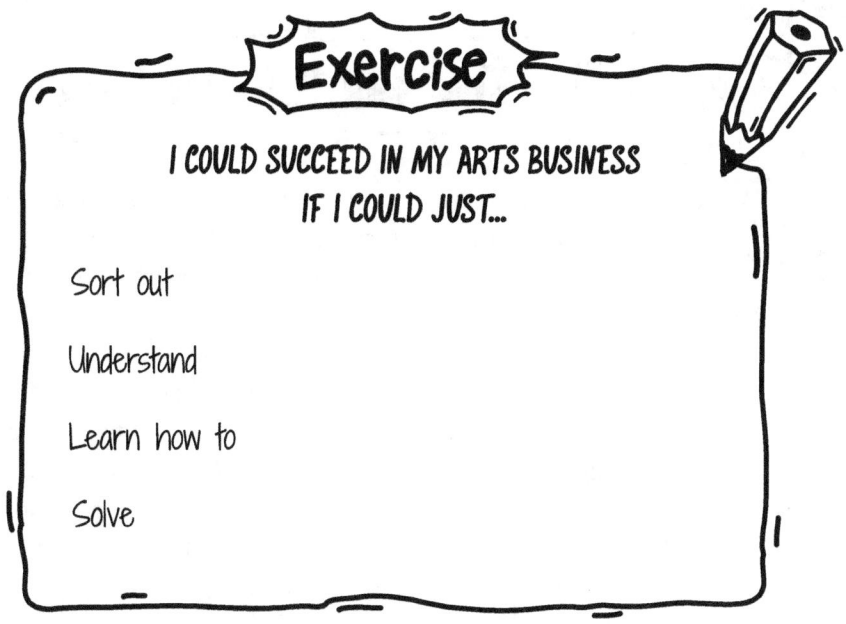

I COULD SUCCEED IN MY ARTS BUSINESS IF I COULD JUST...

Sort out

Understand

Learn how to

Solve

Have a stream of consciousness dialogue with your internal self, with your intuition. Use these four prompts to start writing.

Find a clean page in a journal that you have set aside for your arts business.

Say to yourself, **"I could succeed in my arts business if I could just sort out..."** *and complete the sentence.*

Then take the second prompt, **"I could succeed in my arts business if I could just understand..."** *and fill in the rest of the sentence.*

And take the third prompt, **"I could succeed in my arts business if I could just learn how to..."** *and finish the sentence.*

And take the fourth prompt, **"I could succeed in my arts business if I could just solve..."** *and finish the sentence.*

Again, do not edit as you write. Do not let your brain think too much. Let your intuition complete the sentences rather than your logical mind.

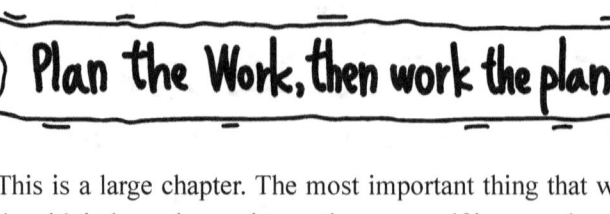

Plan the Work, then work the plan

This is a large chapter. The most important thing that we do with independent artists such as yourself is to teach you to plan the work, then work the plan. We understand plans, and often we use plans when we make our art. Take for example a theatre production. As a card-carrying Equity director, I know that there's an extraordinary plan created to get me and the cast from the first rehearsal to opening night. An awesome stage manager helps me develop a plan that guarantees that we will arrive fully prepared for opening night. With that plan in place, I can come in to work and just work the plan. But if there's no plan, we'll never hit opening night. Well, this same ability that I have as a director to plan a production can be used to plan my arts business. And it was hard for me (at first) to do that. And I know that it has been hard for every artist to understand and appreciate the value of planning.

Before you go to the grocery store, if you take five minutes out to plan the shopping list, you can be very efficient once you get there. You can save time and money. You planned the work, and then you worked the plan. You didn't wander around the store trying to put together the plan at the same time as trying to do doing the shopping. The weird part is that we don't make use of the benefits of planning when it comes to our arts business.

Planning shifts you from being reactive to being proactive. Some of us feel that our careers are in the hands of the fates. It's up to destiny whether we're going to be successful or not. We become very good at being

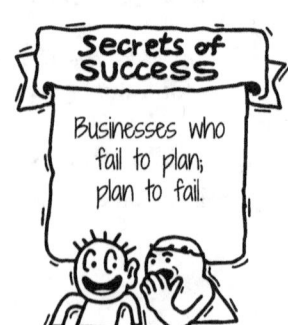

Secrets of Success

Businesses who fail to plan, plan to fail.

reactive. I spoke to an artist just the other day whose life was going along merrily, because she had seized an opportunity to create murals in schools. One day the Provincial Arts Council announced that they were changing the focus of their funding. She was suddenly out of business. Planning would have shifted her arts business from being reactive to proactive.

When you create a plan, your conscious mind understands what it will take to get there. And your subconscious mind helps you notice and recognize all the resources the plan will require.

You know that when you need something to create an artwork, it sort of magically materializes. That's because you've sent a message to your subconscious to be on the lookout for the thing that's going to bring you feelings of satisfaction. Your subconscious is your best friend and wants you to succeed. You help it help you by creating a plan and stating the goal for it.

Sometimes we come up against artists who resist planning because they say, "I'm too busy to plan." Well, here's a rule of life:

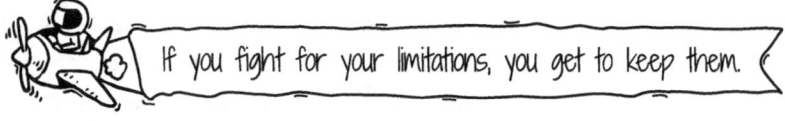

If you fight for your limitations, you get to keep them.

If you're going to live a life that's too busy to do some planning, if you enjoy running around, being frantic, being busy, well, you'll get to stay that way. If that's what you enjoy, your subconscious is being trained that way. It will assume, "That's what you enjoy. So, I'm going to help you to remain busy. I'm going to make sure you're always running around frantically. Because clearly, that's what gives you feelings of satisfaction."

OK, let's back up a bit. I think it might be helpful to understand why we resist planning by examining how most of us ended up as an artist with a business. We typically never intended to have an arts business, so we never planned for it.

Another reason that we don't plan is that we value freedom. We don't want to be locked in. The reason we are a solo entrepreneur is that we value freedom and flexibility. We want to decide by ourselves what we do. And a plan feels like a constraint. But I'm here to tell you that your plan is the dynamic result of gathering all your wisdom to hit a goal and to continue towards success. You can change the plan, because you created it. You're not locked in. Your plan enables your success. Your fantastic artistic skill has gotten you to where you are today. To get beyond today, you need a plan.

It's important to realize that artistic skill does not equal business skill.

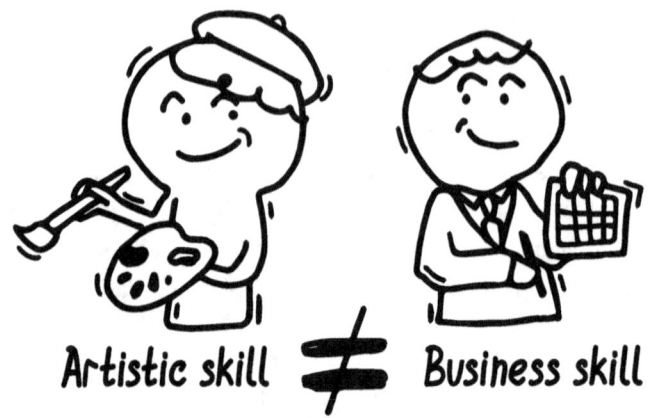

You've invested time, money, and energy to perfect your talent. Now it's time to invest the same time, energy, and money to learn the business skills that you need to be successful and live the life you want to live. This chapter is all about one of those business skills: planning. This chapter also helps you recognize some other business skills that you need to develop in order to thrive.

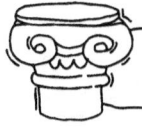 Researching your industry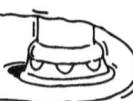

Before you launch into a project or a new business, do some research. I bet you, someone has done this before. You can learn from what they've done. This skill is called modelling. You model your steps on the steps they took, the habits they have, the behaviour they exhibited, the thoughts they had, and the actions they took. When you use that as a model, you're going to develop a similar result. To use successes in your industry or your niche as models is a guaranteed way to get further faster.

Go now.

Do some research.

Find artists who've achieved what you'd like to achieve.

Figure out what steps they took.

Imagine the thoughts they had and the actions they took.

Then do your version of the same.

Remember the Medicine Wheel of Beliefs in Chapter 3? If you can figure out how someone who has the results that you want got there, you can get there the same way.

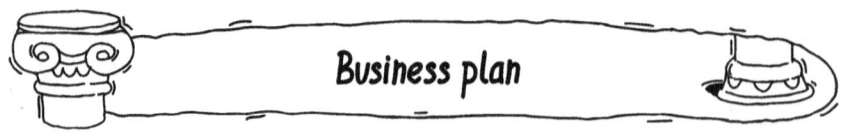

Business plan

A lot of artists come to us because they've heard that they need a business plan. And they phone up and say, "I need a business plan. People tell me I need a business plan." Well, it's true. But I also say,

> You don't need a business plan, you need a plan for your business.

When you're developing a plan for your business, there are three things that I think are important.

Number 1. Have a written plan.

Without a written plan, your arts business is merely a dream. It doesn't have to be a book, but you need a few pages that outline specific objectives. Identify some strategies that you're going to deploy. Figure out the finances. And sketch out some sales and marketing ideas. You need to write this stuff down. You can't just think about it. You need to put it on paper.

Number 2. Don't marry the plan.

Every great military general in history has known that even the best laid plan must sometimes be thrown in the fire when the bullets start flying. Well, the same with the plan for your business. This document you wrote is only the record of your plan. It's only you trying to map out what you need, articulate some goals, set some targets, and understand your business. You wrote it. You can change it. No one's going to hold you to it. The plan is just an awesome tool.

Number 3. Keep your ego in check and listen to others.

Advisors and coaches are crucial to your success. You need people to bounce ideas off, to inspect what you're doing, and to push you to greater accomplishments. Many of us need someone holding us accountable for what we're committing to do. This is planning for your business. Don't take things personally and beware of emotional reactions. Don't let your ego take control.

Working with advisors and getting a coach will help you plan the business. If you're keen on a creating a long formal written document, go for it.

If this is your first business plan, let me explain that a basic business plan answers four questions.

1. **What is the service or product being sold?**

   Just explain it. This is what the business is about. My business is about creating X.

2. **How viable is the business?**

   Remember viability. Is there a market for it? Do you still have the desire to do it? Your business plan document answers this question.

3. **How does the business operate?**

   What's your business structure? Is it all up to you? Do you have collaborators? How does the business actually operate? How do you market your product or service?

4. **What are the finances?**

   How much money does this business generate? How much money could this business generate? Where does the money come from? How is the business financed? Who pays for things?

These are the four questions that a business plan asks and answers.

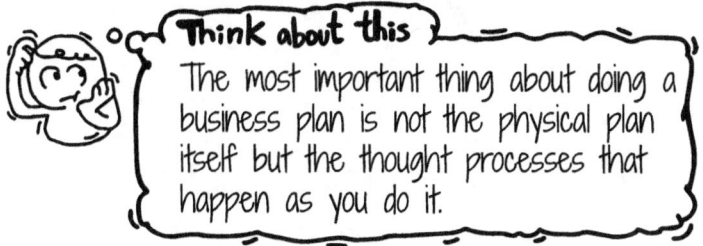

Think about this

The most important thing about doing a business plan is not the physical plan itself but the thought processes that happen as you do it.

Go and develop a much more comprehensive business plan if you want. But I would start with a document that answers just those four questions.

I started this part of the chapter by discussing the need to plan for your business rather than creating a business plan, and that's what I meant. Plan for your business. Go through the process of writing down the answers to these questions, and you'll end up with a business plan.

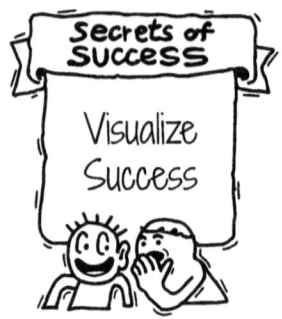

This idea echoes the beginning of the book, where I talked about having the mindset of someone who believes that you can succeed. Part of believing that you can succeed is being able to visualise your success. You have a powerful imagination and a strong connection to your intuition. Put both to work and use visualization techniques.

When you see something or imagine something you want, that image or idea switches on your emotional centre, and you feel a strong desire for it. And that sets your subconscious mind off to gather all the necessary resources and make all the connections that you need. Visualisation aligns your conscious mind and your subconscious mind toward successful completion of what you want.

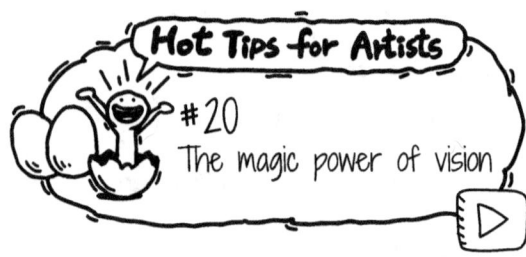

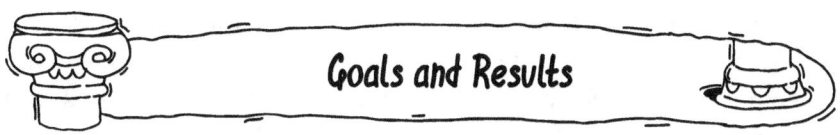

Goals and Results

The best part of planning is clarifying your goals and results. To get familiar with the idea of goals and results, do this exercise.

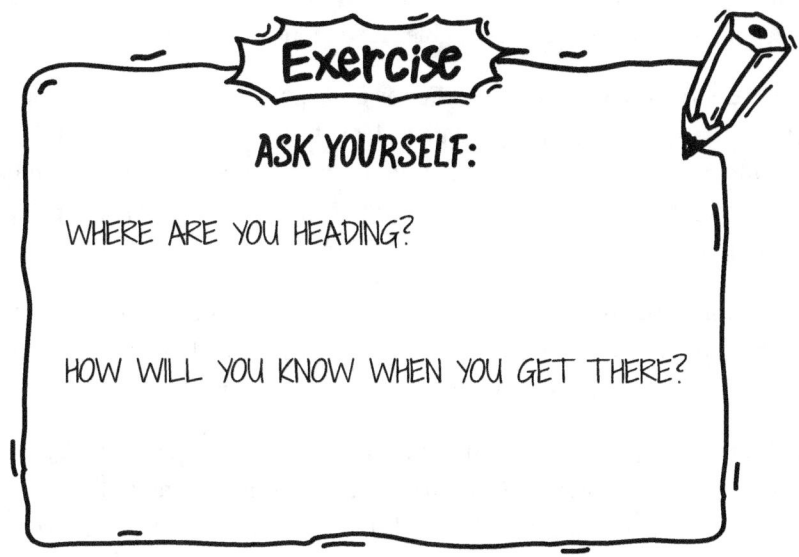

Exercise

ASK YOURSELF:

WHERE ARE YOU HEADING?

HOW WILL YOU KNOW WHEN YOU GET THERE?

Yep! This is another exercise in which you're going to have a dialogue with your intuition and your imagination.

Answer this question: **"Where am I heading?"**

> *Describe it.*
>
> *What's your success going to look like?*
>
> *What are its components?*
>
> *What does it include?*

Then, answer the next question: **"How will I know when I get there?"**

> *What will you see that's different from what you see now?*
>
> *What will you hear yourself saying to yourself?*
>
> *What will you hear other people saying around you?*
>
> *What will you have then that you don't have now?*
>
> *What will you be doing then that you are not doing now?*

The answers to these questions will let you know that you've arrived at your goal. Most artists set out hoping for success. But how will you know when you arrive at your measure of success unless you articulate it? That's what this exercise is designed to do.

Goals are essential for business success. Learn how to set goals. Learn how to write them down. The method that I have developed for artists includes three things: It is specific, measurable, and emotional.

Your goal needs to be specific. For example, X number of dollars from X activity. Be specific. Generalized goals like, "I want to be famous" are very difficult to attain. Be specific. What does it mean to be famous? You might say, "I want to have an article written about myself in the local newspaper." Try to be as specific as you can.

Your goal needs to be measurable. If your goals involve money, state the numbers. How many dollars? Another way to be measurable is to pick a date. You could say, "I want $10,000 in sales by the end of next month."

And, above all, your goal must be emotional. You're an artist. You are in the emotion business. If your goal does not excite you and fill you with desire, you're not going to achieve it. If there's no pressure or desire, you're not going to reach your goal.

Understand the universal law:

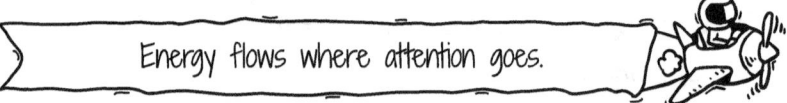

Energy flows where attention goes.

You want to have your goal clearly stated, written down, and posted on the wall, because you want your attention to go toward that goal. You want your attention to go to that piece of paper on the

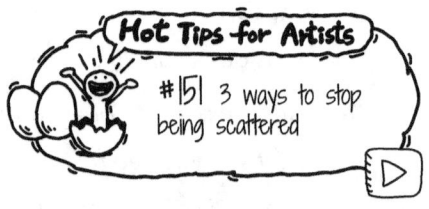

Hot Tips for Artists

#151 3 ways to stop being scattered

wall that states your specific, measurable and emotional goal. Every time you read it, your energy is going to flow in that direction.

Here's a secret about how goals work with artists. Because you have such a powerful imagination and a hard-wired connection to your intuition, visualizing your intended results works better than setting goals to motivate you and keep you on track. If you want to accelerate your progress ten times, you need to visualize success as well as your future results.

To visualize your results, you jump forward in your imagination to the moment in the future occurring immediately after you have achieved your goal. Set your internal time travel guidance system to arrive one minute after you've achieved the goal. Then look around and see what you see. Experience the feeling of having achieved the goal. Hear what you're saying to yourself or what others are saying. Add as many senses to your experience as you can. Make this as real as you can in your imagination, and it will create a powerful anchor to draw you to that moment.

While we're on the subject of planning, there are a couple of other things that require advance planning. Think about these things now.

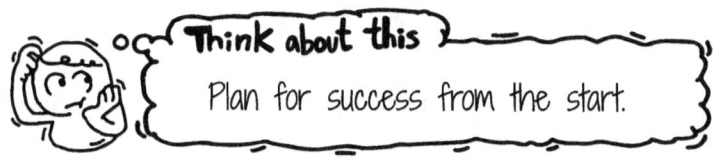

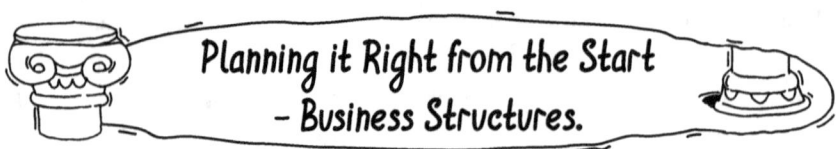

Planning it Right from the Start – Business Structures.

It's important for you to plan the right business structure from the very beginning. Plan for success right from the start. What's the best business structure for you to have? Here are some options that you have for setting up your business structure.

Sole trader

Most of you will start out as a sole trader or sole proprietor. This business structure is simple and cheap to set up. Usually, you can operate under your own name or some other registered business name. You control and manage the business. You get the profits and you are responsible for all debts and liabilities.

Partnership

Consider if a partnership is right for your business. It's a legal structure formed when two or more (up to 20) people go into business together. It's created using some form of a written partnership agreement. The partners operate under their own names or a registered business name.

Incorporated

Another business structure that you could consider right from the start is an incorporated structure. That's when you set up a company. These come in a variety of flavours: C-Corp, or an S-Corp, an LLC, a PTY LTD. Depending on the country you live in, there are various incorporated structures you can use. There are certain tax benefits for a company. If you can imagine that your business will someday provide way more money than you personally need to live on, you might consider one of these structures. They are complex and more expensive to register.

Understand that shareholders own the company and directors run the company. The incorporated entity is responsible for all its debts and liabilities.

Shareholders are exposed to limited liability to pay debts. This structure is registered with the government. It's something to you might want to research thoroughly, because it might be the structure appropriate for you. Be prepared to move into this structure when you need to.

Not for profit

Another business structure that's worth considering in the arts is the not-for-profit structure. In Australia, this can either be an Incorporated Association or a Company Limited by Guarantee. They are relatively easy and inexpensive to set up in Australia and Canada, a bit more complicated in the USA. Not-for-profits are incorporated in a specific state or in a specific province. You're governed by rules of purpose through an elected committee of management, sometimes called your Board. And you must lodge annual statements.

Consider forming a not-for-profit entity if your vision is bigger than you can realize by yourself. If you can imagine a day when you leave the business and they hire someone else to replace you and the work will still continue, consider setting up a not-for-profit.

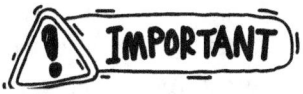

A not-for-profit does not mean that the business cannot make a profit. You can absolutely make a profit. Setting up your business as a not-for-profit just means that members, sometimes considered shareholders, do not receive dividends. They do not receive the profits. The profits of the business cannot be distributed to the members or the shareholders. All the profits of the business must go back into the business to achieve the aims and ideals of the business. Typically, if you are the founding artist of a not-for-profit, you start out taking a very small salary. But as the business grows and makes more money, your salary increases. And that's perfectly fine. The profits from the company can go back to generating the artistic product and service. And if that requires hiring more artists or increasing an artist's fees, that's perfectly acceptable.

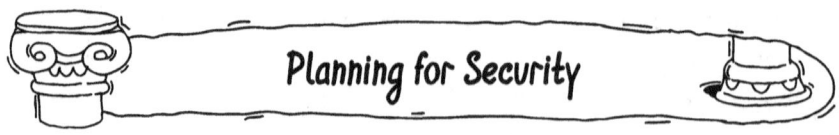

Planning for Security

At some point, you must accept the responsibility of planning for the security of your arts business. There are really four kinds of insurance that I think you should be aware of.

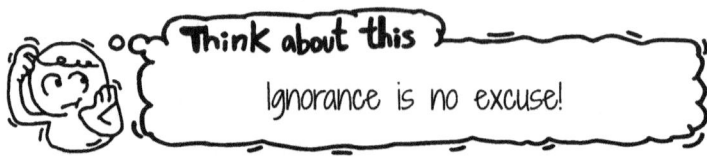

Think about this

Ignorance is no excuse!

1. **Public liability.** This covers the interaction between your business and the public. It does not cover the interactions between your business and employees or volunteers. Those are different kinds of insurance. The only thing this type of insurance covers is the interaction between your products and service, your business, your events, and the public.

2. **Employees and volunteer cover.** This insurance covers the interaction between your arts business and your volunteers or your employees. When you have employees, this type of insurance is sometimes combined with Workers' Compensation Insurance.

3. **Property, goods, and equipment.** Your business might use expensive equipment. You might need to transport expensive equipment. Property, goods, and equipment might be an insurance that you want to carry.

4. **Professional indemnity.** This insurance is something that you should consider if you're incorporated or in the not-for-profit sector. If you're teaching classes, if you're advising other people about how to conduct their lives, how to develop their work, professional indemnity might be something that you should consider.

We're in the emotion business and in the ideas business. We generate things that never existed before. To effectively use and protect your ideas, it's important to do a little bit of planning around IP, (intellectual property) and copyright.

Let's start with copyright. Copyright is the right to own, reproduce, communicate, publish, perform, and adapt your creative works. Copyright is automatic and applies from the time of creation of a work in a physical form.

The creator of an artistic work is automatically its copyright holder. Copyright only protects tangible expressions. It does not protect ideas. Use the 'drop it on your foot' test. If you can drop it on your foot, you can copyright it. If you can't drop it on your foot, it's probably intellectual property.

The copyright symbol © does not need to be used to establish that the work is under copyright. It's a good idea to use it though, to send a signal to people that you take yourself and your work seriously and that you know your rights.

To possess copyright over something, you must create it and hold it in some tangible form. For example, if you've written a song but it's never been transcribed onto paper, recorded onto a disk, or put onto a thumb drive— something that you could drop on your foot—it's not eligible for copyright.

Ideas, goodwill, fame, processes, secret recipes, experience. These things are not in a tangible form. You can't drop them on your foot. They are intellectual property. And there are different things that you can do to protect intellectual property, of the most important is to put them in a tangible form whenever possible.

An unpleasant realization that comes up quite regularly in the arts is when you or your artwork gets photographed for the press and you discover, surprise! The photographer owns the copyright to that image, not you. Even though that image is of you and of your work, the photographer owns the copyright. They have created a thing that can be dropped on your foot. Your sculpture or your painting can also be dropped on your foot. But that particular image of you or your work is owned by the person who created it, and you have to get permission to use it.

Another question that comes up is, "Can I use someone else's work?" Only if you have permission. If someone created something and it's in tangible form, they own the copyright to it. You must get permission to use it. If you think it's worth using, you can bet they think it's worth protecting. There are many other things that relate to this topic, but that's a whole other book. If you're concerned about using and protecting your ideas or using the ideas and art of others, you might want to investigate Moral Rights as well as a companion to Copyright called Creative Commons. I leave it to you to just Google those. I'm not going to dive into them in this chapter.

I think I've helped you understand why it's important to plan the work and then relax and work the plan. It sets you and your business up for success. It keeps you proactive, not reactive. When you try to be the chief worker and the CEO of your business simultaneously, it causes stress, frustration, and burnout. Set aside time to be the CEO and to plan the work. Then you can go into the studio or into the rehearsal hall and just do the work. Just follow the plan. Enjoy being the artist. Take the pressure off trying to juggle being the CEO and the artist at the same time. Plan the work, then work the plan.

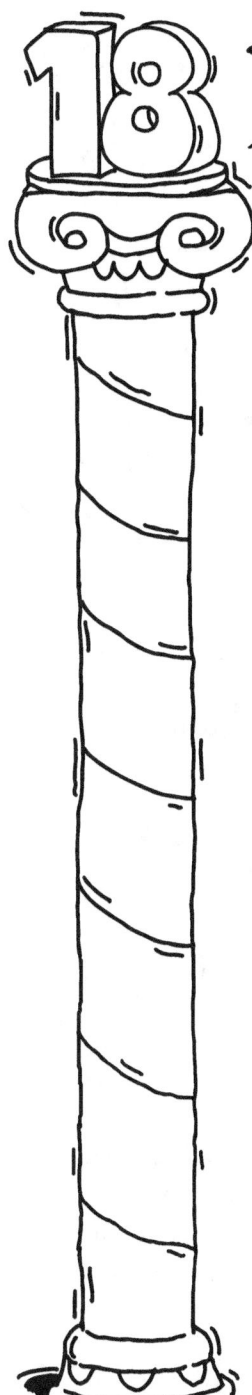

Task management

Working smarter means being able to handle more tasks and being efficient with managing all those tasks. As your business grows and you get busier, you rely on lists to organize your tasks. But that same old list system isn't going to work for your growing business. I bet you can relate to this situation: it's time to revise your to-do list, and when you write the new list on a new piece of paper you notice that some items are getting copied from list to list. They never seem to get crossed off. That's because those things are jobs. They are not tasks. They don't belong on a to-do list. They're too big to be ticked off any list. They are jobs masquerading as tasks.

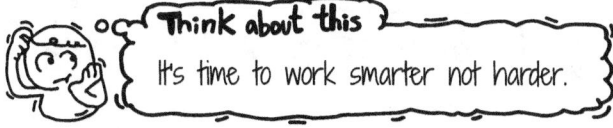

Think about this

It's time to work smarter not harder.

One of the things you need to do in learning to manage the workload is to make sure that everything on your to-do-list is a task. Something is a job when it's composed of multiple tasks, and it never gets crossed off your to-do list. It must be broken down into manageable, bite-sized tasks. For ease of understanding, I define a task as something that can be completed in one sitting of ideally 30 minutes (maybe up to 2 hours, if you have that sort of focus and stamina). Each task needs to be something that you can complete in one sitting, in one focused burst of energy. Getting jobs off your to-do list and breaking them down into manageable tasks is one of the first skills in managing your business.

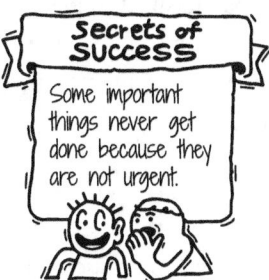

Secrets of Success

Some important things never get done because they are not urgent.

Lots of things that will propel our business are important, but they don't get completed because they aren't urgent.

Here's a 4-quadrant to-do list that I encourage all artists to use.

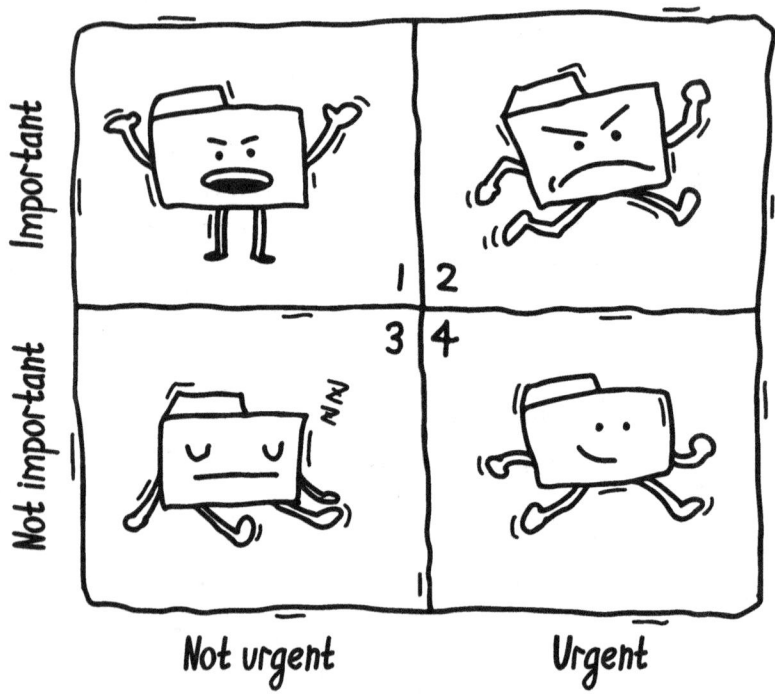

Reproduce this diagram in large size and put it somewhere on a wall where you can see it every day. Each of these sections should be the size of one sheet of paper or larger. We are visual/kinaesthetic learners. It is important that this 4-quadrant to-do list takes up a lot of surface area.

The next step is to do a total brain dump of all the things you need to do on a separate sheet of paper. Take everything on this 'mother to-do list' and write each item on a sticky note. Look at it attentively and make sure that it can be achieved in one sitting. If it can't, it's a job and needs to get broken down into steps.

If you find a job, ask, "What's the first step that needs to be taken that I could do in 30 minutes? What's the next step after that?" Reduce it to its tasks. Put each task on a sticky note.

Now every sticky note has a task on it. Look at each sticky note and ask, "Hmm, how important is this?" Then hold it over the 4-quadrant list. Move it up and down the scale of importance and determine its level of importance. Trust your intuition to feel where it needs to be. Next, allow your intuition to carry it over to the right. How urgent is this? If it's very urgent, it's going to keep moving to the right. Once you find where it's going to live, between urgency and importance, place the note on the chart. Repeat this with all your tasks on your sticky notes.

Let me help you understand the four quadrants.

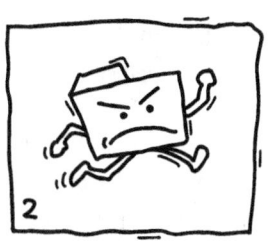

Quadrant 2:

This quadrant contains the things that are both important and urgent. They are probably going to get taken care of. You don't really need to devote much energy or focus to them. Things that are in this quadrant just need to be managed. Time must be scheduled to complete them, that's all.

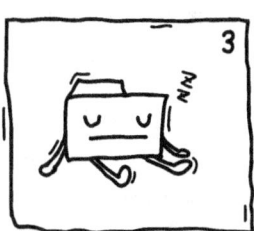

Quadrant 3:

These are things that are not important and not urgent. You want to try to delegate or eliminate them. The reality of being in business is that sometimes things just don't get done. If no harm will come from not doing one of these things, just eliminate it. You just need to let go of some of these things.

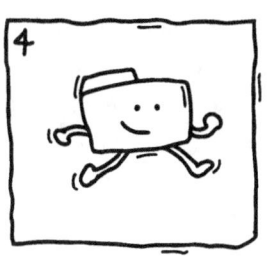

Quadrant 4:

Things that are in this quadrant, not important but urgent, are the ones to be wary of. These are the time suckers. These are the people that have asked you for a favour. These are the needs of THEM (Chapter 8). Beware of things that are in this quadrant. Try to delegate them, get rid of them, or complete them quickly. They are urgent for someone else, not for you. Try to control this section.

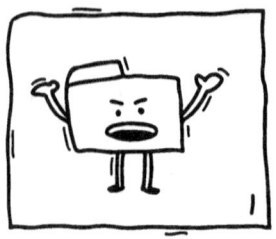

Quadrant 1:

This is the most important quadrant: the things that are important but not urgent. The tasks in this quadrant are the things that are going to propel your arts business the most. This is also where some sneaky jobs are hiding. Things that are important but not urgent are things that will get you further. They are not urgent, because you don't know when or if they're going to work. These are things that you want to try. These are people that you want to make connections with. They're not urgent, but they're really important. And as you start to get control of your day, your week, and your month, and your year, you MUST schedule time for the things that are in this quadrant.

Your old to-do list was just a list of urgent things. It wasn't a to-do list designed to propel your business. It was just a way for you to manage deadlines of urgent things so that you didn't forget them. When you see a more comprehensive to-do list on the wall in the 4-quadrant structure, you begin to think of things that will propel the business. You begin to look for things in quadrant one. "What are these important things that haven't been on my to-do list but have been at the back of my mind? What are the things that I know are really important?"

As the CEO of your arts business, it's vital for you to be doing things that are important for your arts business but that are not necessarily urgent. And it is important to include these tasks in your schedule every day and every week.

It's time to get better at task management by making sure that you're dealing with tasks and not jobs. Break jobs down into tasks. Understand the level of importance versus the level of urgency for every task. Spend your time and your energy on things that are important for your business. It's time to stop rushing around, just being busy, handling only the things that are urgent.

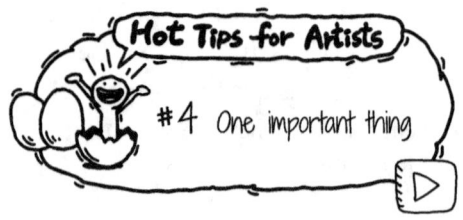

Hot Tips for Artists

#4 One important thing

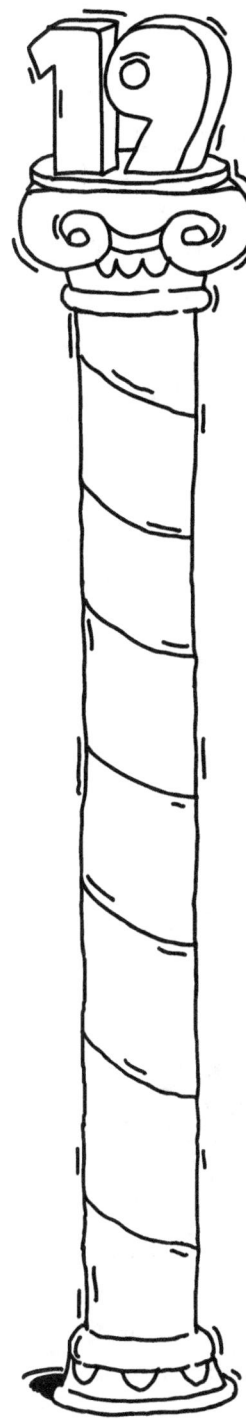

Time management

As you develop your planning and productivity, it's important to understand how to better manage your time. As you get busier and there are more demands on you to produce more work and to manage the business more effectively, it becomes critical to learn to manage your time. The key to time management for artists is doing what is important first. Do the things that will lead you to achieve your goals first, because there's always going to be some interruption that will derail your day.

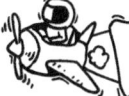

Start your day working on the business, not in the business.

Time management is also about choice management. You must control what you do with your time, so make sure that you are the one choosing what you are doing. If you allow other people to control your time, you are not managing your time, and you will burn out really quickly.

The three Ps of time management that I find most effective for artists are: **prioritize, plan** and **perform.**

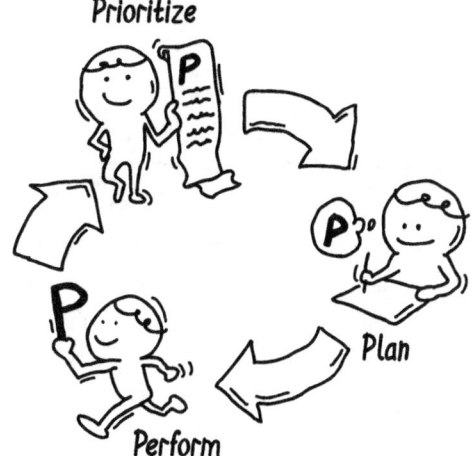

Prioritize

Plan

Perform

We've looked at Plan in Chapter 18 and we've looked at Prioritize in the previous chapter. Let's look at the final P—Perform. There are literally thousands of helpful hints, lessons, exercises, and even some mobile apps to help you achieve peak performance in your work, in your life, even in your leisure time, and I encourage you to explore them. This chapter contains what I've seen works for artists. These are tips and tricks that have proved effective with hundreds of artists.

There are several things that keep you from using your time efficiently and performing at your optimal level. In my experience, artists lose time because of these six:

1. perfectionism,

2. multitasking,

3. procrastination,

4. interruptions,

5. looking for things,

6. second-guessing your decisions.

1. **Perfectionism.** I call this time black hole 'perfection paralysis'. We don't move, we don't complete, simply because it isn't perfect. Remember that in business we say,

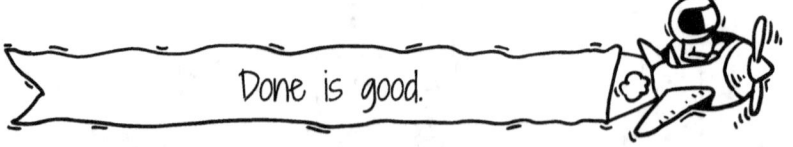

Done is good.

It's important to reach for excellence, but remember that 'done' is good. 'Out into the market' is better. Perfectionism is the number-one time trap for artists. We can spend way too much time trying to perfect something, trying to make all the fine adjustments possible. At a certain point, get it to market—done is good.

2. Multitasking should make sense to you as a source of time loss, because energy flows where attention goes. If your attention is moving between multiple things, they all get a little bit of energy, and often you waste or lose time shifting your focus.

3. Procrastination is something you need to tackle. Your first job is to figure out why you are procrastinating.

There are lots of tools out there to overcome procrastination. But here is the ABCDE of tackling procrastination:

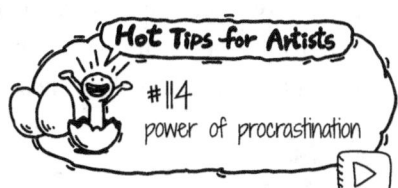

A. **Change your language.** *When something needs to get done, stop saying, "Oh, I have to. Oh, I should." Those are excuses and they create energy and emotion that does not move forward and isn't progressive. Start changing your language to, "I'm choosing to. I've decided to." That's empowering language. These phrases propel you toward completing the task.*

B. **Break it down.** *We've talked about this before. If it's a job, you procrastinate because it's too big. If it's a task, you can just sit down and get at it. Only if you can imagine and believe that you will complete it will you start it.*

C. **Take the first step of only 30 minutes.** *If you're procrastinating because you don't know how long it will take to complete the task, or if you have enough time, set a time limit on the task. Give it 30 minutes. When 30 minutes are up, you can choose to spend more time working or stop.*

D. **Set a deadline and be accountable.** *If you have no deadline for something, you can procrastinate forever. Get an accountability buddy or a coach. Ask someone to help you by holding you accountable for finishing the task.*

E. **Reward the behaviour you would like to continue.** *When you don't procrastinate and just get on with it instead, give yourself a reward. Take a moment to enjoy that good feeling of having done it. That little reward sends a signal to your subconscious that says, "Oh, I actually like it when I complete something better than I like procrastinating and the feeling of looming obligations hanging over my head."*

Back to how we lose time…

4. **Interruptions,** both external and internal. Internal interruptions are a close relative of procrastination. These interruptions also bear a striking resemblance to 'The Shiny Object Syndrome'. Sometimes, internally, you're procrastinating. You're looking for some new idea, some other shiny object to interrupt your flow and occupy your time. Sometimes, externally, you allow yourself to be interrupted. You allow people to derail your day, to use your time, to interrupt you in the studio or in the rehearsal hall. Don't allow those interruptions.

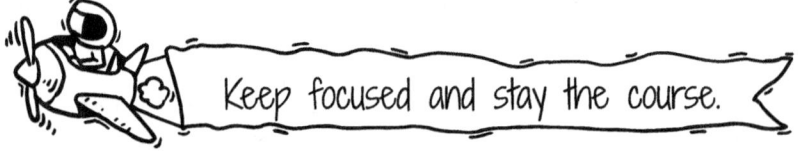

Keep focused and stay the course.

5. **Looking for things** loses a lot of time. Are you continually losing time because you don't remember where you put something, particularly on the computer? It's important to set up good filing systems so that you don't waste time looking for things. It's also important to understand how your computer uses its search function so that you find things quickly using keywords.

6. **Second-guessing your decisions** costs time. Kierkegaard, the philosopher, made a great existential statement, "Whichever you choose, you're going to regret both." And I think that sometimes this is true for artists as well. You second-guess your decisions. Make a decision and move on. You can always correct your course. Stop second-guessing your decisions.

The best habit for ultimate time management is to schedule things. If it isn't in your calendar, then you have not set it as a priority. If it is not in your calendar, then chances are that something else will come up that you're going to deal with instead. You are bullshitting yourself when you say you will do it if it's not in your calendar. Scheduling it in your calendar is more powerful than putting it on your to-do-list.

Another essential habit for Performance is **owning your morning.**

Start your day working ON your business. It's going to set you up for success. It's going to help you to manage your time. If you start your morning by responding to other people, they're controlling your time. You want to be in control and manage your time. And that starts by controlling your morning. Do not start the day by jumping into your email. NO MORE…

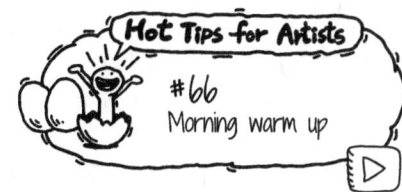

Hot Tips for Artists
#66
Morning warm up

Exercise

Put your hand on your heart right now and repeat this out loud. "I hereby promise that tomorrow, and every day after that, I will take control of my day by checking my email at a time later in the day that suits me and my business best."

If you want to get on top of your time management, owning your morning is critical. Time management works hand in hand with valuing you and valuing your time. Start every working day by reflecting on what you want to achieve, looking at your goals, and visualizing how you want the day to go. Start your working days by choosing to spend time on nurturing you. Time management skills are going to become more and more essential as your business grows.

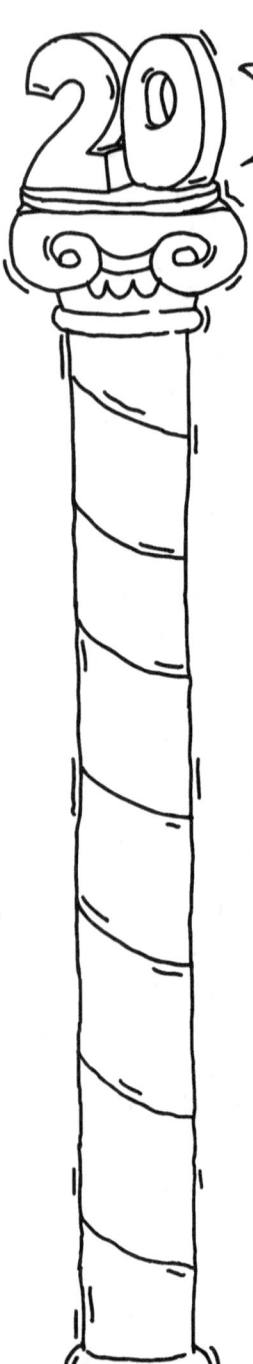

Emotions management

Emotions are great for the creative process, but not so great for keeping your business running. This final chapter is devoted to helping you manage yourself. Understand how to manage the emotions that are essential to the creation of your art. Understand how to manage the emotions that are part of who you are as the CEO and principle artist in your arts business.

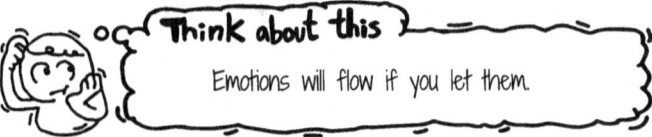

Think about this

Emotions will flow if you let them.

Emotions are not designed to be stuck on or to hang around. They are designed to do the job of shifting your focus and then move on. It's important to feel emotions. It's the way your subconscious mind tells you what you want. Acknowledge the emotion, feel the emotion, then let it flow. We are emotional beings, and we are in the emotion business. Being a good and responsible owner of a small arts business is understanding how to manage your emotions and the emotions of the people that experience our art.

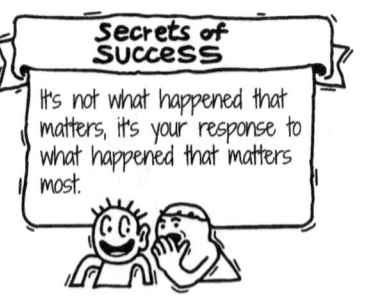

Secrets of Success

It's not what happened that matters, it's your response to what happened that matters most.

Lots of things will happen as you create art and put it out into the world. The important part is not what happened, it's your response to what happens that is important for your business. The way you respond to criticism, the way you respond to success, the way you respond to failure, the way you respond to emotional swings is up to you. How you respond is up to you. Emotions are inevitable. Situations and people will trigger emotions, but you have the choice of how you respond. You are not a victim of your emotions. Your emotions are part of your work. They come, they go, they draw your focus. You take a deep breath and you let them flow. Don't hold them. There are too many of them.

Your job is to respond appropriately to your emotional triggers. When something unexpected happens, a reaction is triggered. But in the split-second before you react, there is an opportunity to make a choice about how you respond. Exert control and learn how to replace the automatic reaction with a contained response. It's more helpful for the business.

If you are constantly reacting to emotions, you're not being very proactive. When you allow some space between an emotional trigger and your response to it, then you are proactive and in control of your business.

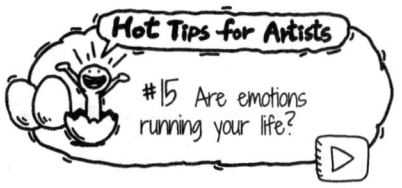

One of the best emotion management tools I can recommend is paying attention to triggers and reactions and observing how they work. For a while, you're just going to notice that a reaction got triggered. And then, pretty soon, your awareness is going to grow and you will begin to exercise choice. You'll say, "Hmm, let's change this automatic habit of trigger and reaction. What if I inserted a pause in the process so I could choose how I want to respond?" And then the next time you feel that trigger, you'll react, but you'll go, "Oh, look, I just did that again." And then the next time it happens, things will seem to slow down… you're going to think, "Oh! This is that thing"—pause, choose a response, execute the response, continue. Then the next time you experience the trigger, you're going to observe yourself saying, "Oh, look. Here's that trigger again. I don't have to react. I can make a different choice." Developing this skill requires education and observation of your emotions. Look back at that Medicine Wheel of Beliefs (Chapter 3). Remember that quite often your emotions are tied to some thoughts that you just had. So, it might be that managing your emotions begins with managing your thoughts, which in turn begins with managing your beliefs.

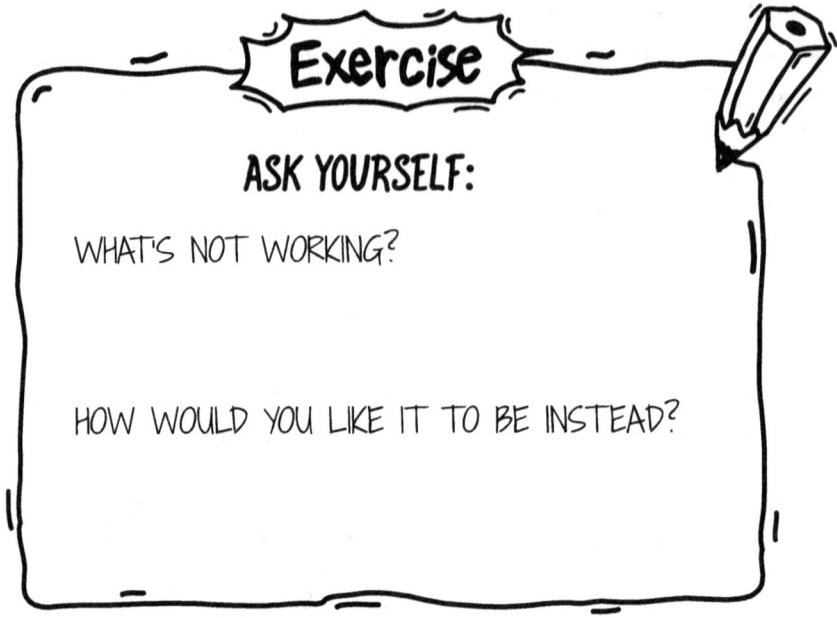

Exercise

ASK YOURSELF:

WHAT'S NOT WORKING?

HOW WOULD YOU LIKE IT TO BE INSTEAD?

Change the way you think and talk about the things that are not working in your business. We're all very good at describing the things that aren't working, talking about the obstacles, sharing the pain, the anxiety, the stress. Sharing what isn't working becomes your story. You create energy around that negative description. This exercise helps you reframe the way you talk about things. Rather than continuing to talk about what's not working, think about how you would like it to be instead.

Write down something that's not working.

Then, write down how would you like it to be instead.

To better manage your emotions, start describing what's going on by using the language of how you would like it to be instead. Stop telling the story of what's not working. Changing your language is one of the things that you can do that will have an immediate effect on your emotional frame. State it the way you want it. Stop talking about how it's not working. Stop putting energy into describing and validating the hardship. Start telling a story that includes language that states it the way you want it and then move in that direction.

Changing your language is part of a triad of skills that you can develop to manage your emotions and to change a negative emotional state into one that is more productive for your arts business.

It is possible for you to change your emotional state by changing your focus, your language, and your physiology.

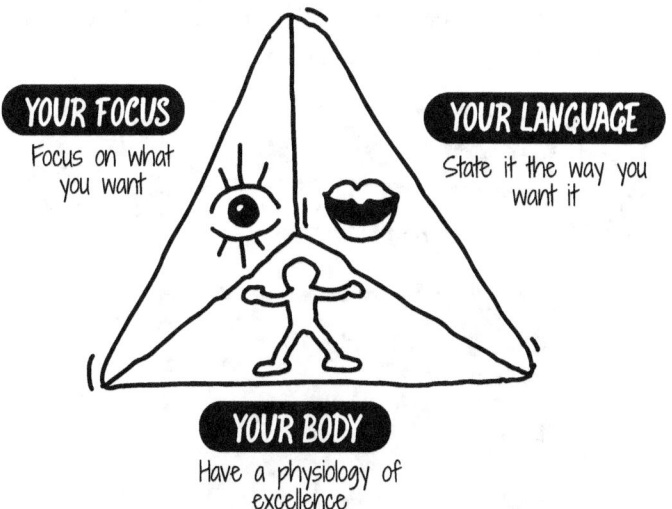

You can change your focus, since what you focus on is totally in your control. You can focus on what you want rather than what you don't want. Your mind works a bit like a search engine. You get what you're looking for. If you type 'poverty' into a search engine, you're going to be surrounded by the world of poverty. If you type 'success' into the search engine, you're going to surrounded by the world of success. Decide to change your focus, just like you're changing your language. If your language is going to change so as to allow you to talk about how you want things to be instead, change your focus in the same way. One of the easiest ways to change your focus is to get back to that gratitude journal I introduced you to in Chapter 3. If you start your day with writing down the things you're grateful for, you've shifted your focus to things that are positive.

Another way to skilfully manage your emotions and change your emotional state is at the physical level. When you change your posture, it changes your emotional state. You can choose to adopt the posture of excellence. Imagine yourself an 'excellent person' and embody that posture. If you're walking around with your head down, your shoulders drooping, your breathing shallow, your eyes on the floor, it's hard to be positive and energized. If you lift your eyes, smile, put your shoulders back, and open your chest, you will shift your emotional state. Try it. It's very hard to walk upright with a posture of pride and sustain a dark, depressed emotional state.

You can manage your emotions by changing your focus, changing your language, and changing your body. Become an expert at shifting your emotional state so that you can manage the emotions that are so vital for the creation of art and the success of your arts business.

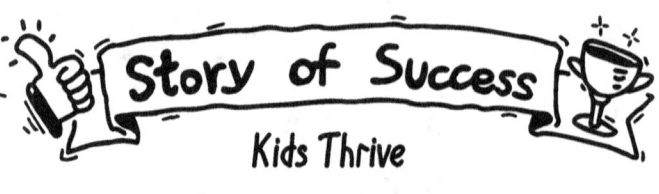

Story of Success
Kids Thrive

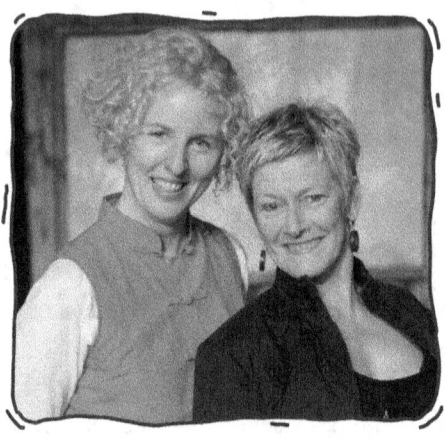

When Andrea Lemon and Andrea Rieniets came into the incubator, they were running in a hamster wheel. They had a small children's music company doing great work empowering kids' lives. They had a couple of shows and did a bit of touring. They were both balancing full-time jobs outside of their art practice. They hit that point as mid-career artists, at which they said, "Well, this is it. It's too hard. Things have to change, or we're going to throw in the towel." They decided to work with us. They clarified their vision, changed their mindset, established a new brand, and built the company around their values. They learned to deliver their message using value-based language and market their art more effectively. They learned to manage their business. They re-engineered their company with a different business structure. They learned to track and manage their expenses. They learned to manage their time, to plan, and to be highly productive. We worked with them to grow the business revenue to the point that they're now turning over a million dollars a year.

They're still doing what they love and still empowering kids and changing the destiny of communities. They've realized that their art is far bigger than just children's music and they have created an entire not-for-profit that is dedicated to this bigger picture. From two women who started a company as a part-time venture, they are now an organisation that employs a team of 15 people, and they've learned to manage those people. They are in a very emotional business. The work that they do with children is profound, and they have developed methods of managing the emotions of the children as well as the emotions of the team. It's all possible, because they made all five of these pillars solid, strong, and capable of supporting the business they have built on top.

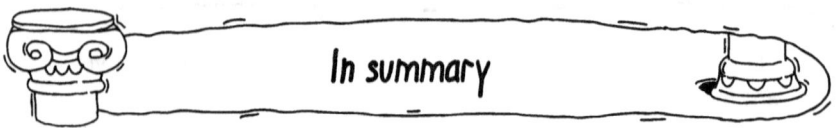

In summary

Building this last pillar of Planning & Productivity is a lifelong endeavour. Every six months, you and your business will be in a slightly different place. Learning to work ON the business is the key to keeping yourself moving forward and growing. Continually improving and developing better habits of productivity is part of the fun. Continuous improvement is the creative process of managing yourself and your business. I encourage you to get help with this last section. Having a coach, attending seminars and classes, and subscribing to podcasts are really important to help you maintain this last pillar of planning and productivity. You need an external perspective. You need someone to bounce ideas off. I encourage you to get support and help, because this fifth pillar requires lots of reflection and some external perspective.

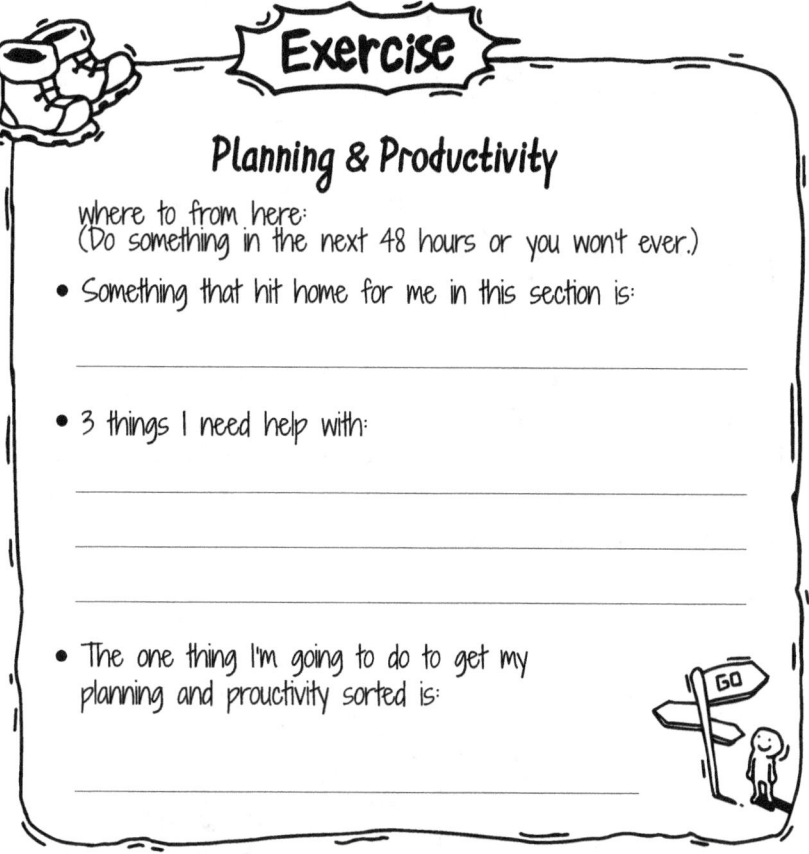

Exercise

Planning & Productivity

where to from here:
(Do something in the next 48 hours or you won't ever.)

- Something that hit home for me in this section is:

_____

- 3 things I need help with:

_____

_____

_____

- The one thing I'm going to do to get my planning and prouctivity sorted is:

_____

Artists before you have identified these top six things from this section as worthy of their focus:

1. write a plan

2. write my goals

3. clean up my to-do list

4. figure out why I procrastinate

5. create a morning ritual

6. say it the way I want it

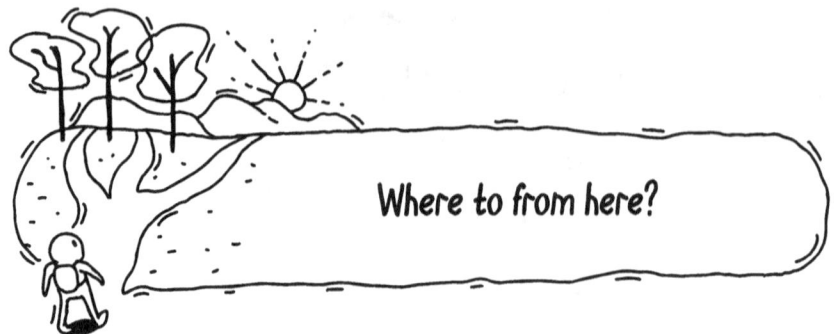

Where to from here?

If you've made it to the end of this book with me, congratulations! Making it to the end of this book, doing the exercises and thinking about your art as a business means that you are destined to be a successful artist in business. You can't un-think this stuff. You've built five strong pillars that can support your business and enable it to grow.

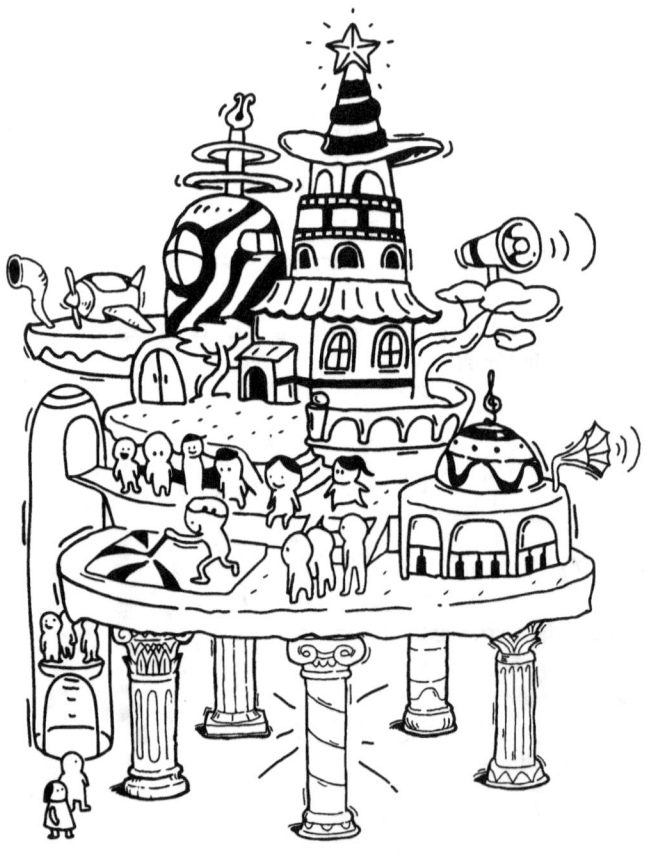

I said when we started this journey together that this book is not a magic bullet. This book can't possibly give you everything you need to know.

This book is not a replacement for our more intensive programs.

If you want to get further faster, contact us about our larger and more intense programs.

This book is also not a replacement for coaching.

The number one thing that will move your arts businesses towards success is working with a coach.

This book is not the end of your learning curve.

There are 92 discrete skills to learn to run your arts business.

Here is a quick diagnostic exercise to help you figure out what to do next.

Exercise

ON A SCALE OF 1-5 ASSESS THE CAPABILITY OF YOUR ARTS PRACTICE TO BE SUCCESSFUL & SUSTAINABLE...

vision & mindset

	not at all 1	2	somewhat 3	4	absolutely 5
I am clear about all the ways I earn money from my art					
I create opportunities for myself and my art					
I believe I will succeed					
SUB-TOTAL					

branding & values

	1	2	3	4	5
I have a clear and compelling vision for my arts business					
I know and use what my customers say about me and my art					
The price I charge includes adequate remuneration for me					
SUB-TOTAL					

marketing & message

	1	2	3	4	5
I know my primary niche market					
I have a database of my customers					
I know the benefits I and my art provide to my customers					
SUB-TOTAL					

money & finance

	1	2	3	4	5
I keep good financial records					
I categorise and track my business expenses					
I set financial goals					
SUB-TOTAL					

planning & productivity

	1	2	3	4	5
I have (and am following) my business plan					
My time is efficiently scheduled and managed					
I can see, feel and hear my success					
SUB-TOTAL					

_____

TOTAL

WHAT DOES IT MEAN?

15–39: You would benefit from a training program to build your business.

40–53: You are ready to learn the missing pieces that will make your arts practice a successful arts buiness.

54–67: You're on the right track; get a coach to help you improve a few things.

68–75: You are doing great!

I want to wrap up by thanking you for being an artist. Seriously, thank you. No one forced this life on you. You chose it. You chose to follow the muse. You chose to honour your gift and pursue the wild path of creation and discovery. I want to salute that choice. Artists are the most valuable citizens we've got. You stretch minds, open hearts, and change lives. You and your art are powerful. The contribution you make to the world is vital. This has not been easy. You've invested your time, your heart, and your money as well as countless other resources in creating art that makes people's lives deeper, richer, and more exciting.

Keep going – the world needs you. At least once a week my heart breaks when I meet an artist who retreats from greatness and decides not to step out of their comfort zone.

If there was a magic elixir I could create that would get you from where you are now to where you could be after you drank it, you would instantly

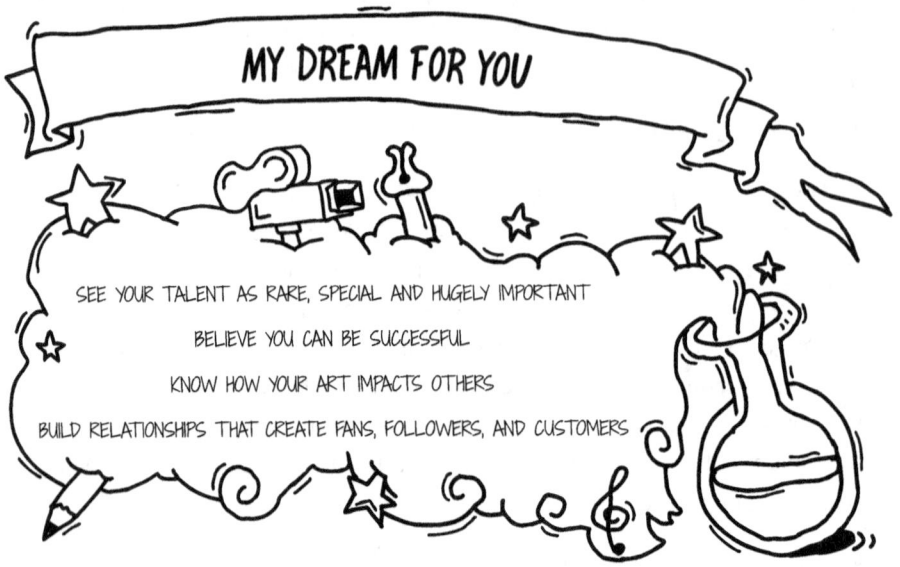

MY DREAM FOR YOU

SEE YOUR TALENT AS RARE, SPECIAL AND HUGELY IMPORTANT

BELIEVE YOU CAN BE SUCCESSFUL

KNOW HOW YOUR ART IMPACTS OTHERS

BUILD RELATIONSHIPS THAT CREATE FANS, FOLLOWERS, AND CUSTOMERS

Alas, there's no magic elixir, but you can have all these things.

I love the fact that we've created many ways to help every artist thrive, no matter where you are or what you create.

With all my heart, thank you for choosing a life that can be hard and joyous and is often a little difficult to explain.

Sincerely, with the utmost admiration and respect, I thank you for being an artist.

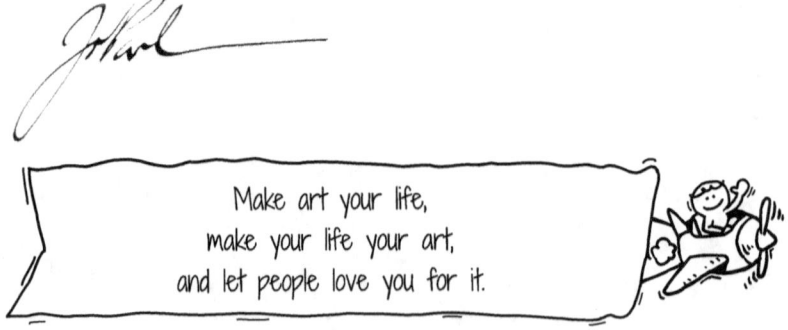

Make art your life,
make your life your art,
and let people love you for it.

About the author

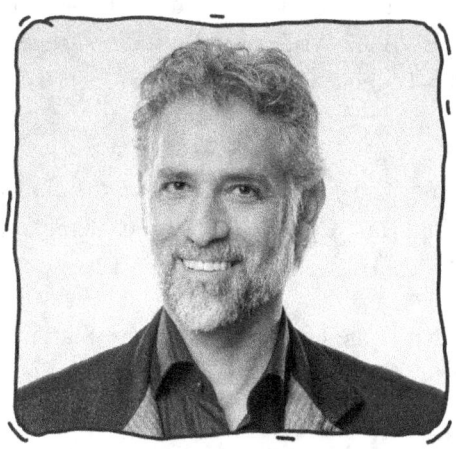

*Author, Producer, Director, Designer, Educator, and an
Arts Business Consultant*

John Paul is an author, producer, director, designer, educator, and a highly sought-after arts business consultant. He is a successful artist entrepreneur whose greatest strength is having lived the artist experience.

As the CEO and co-founder of Auspicious Arts Incubator, John Paul travels extensively around Australia as well as the US and Canada, helping independent artists, organisations, and venues make more money by learning to use value-based language for their marketing and communications. He has a long history of producing and directing theatre, film, festivals, and site-specific events, from the 1984 Olympic Arts Festival in Los Angeles to the International Puppet Carnival in Melbourne.

In 2014, he launched the Artists Transformation School, an online resource that teaches artists everything they need to know about how to turn their creative passion into a business. Additionally, he launched the Artist's Mojo to help artists get out of their own way and find greater success.

Throughout his career, he has worked with more than 3,000 artists, arts organisations, local and state governments, and art centres. He has transformed the lives and careers of individuals in a wide range of disciplines, including those in fine art, sculpture, music, jewellery, photography, writing, acting, dance, illustration, filmmaking, and animation.

John Paul's professional associations include the Canadian Actors Equity, the Society of Children's Book Writers and Illustrators, Americans for the Arts, the Creative Skills Training Council, and the Deer Tribe Metis Medicine Society.

He has travelled and worked all over Australia, the United States, Canada, the United Kingdom, Bali, Costa Rica, Mexico, Denmark, Hawaii, Ireland, Scotland, South Africa, Botswana, Greece, and Turkey.

John Paul Fischbach is the author of 'No More Starving Artists', a guide written by an artist for artists, and lives in Victoria, Australia.

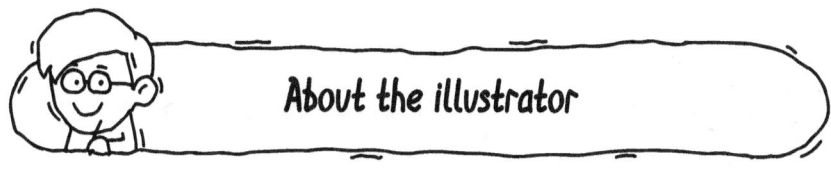

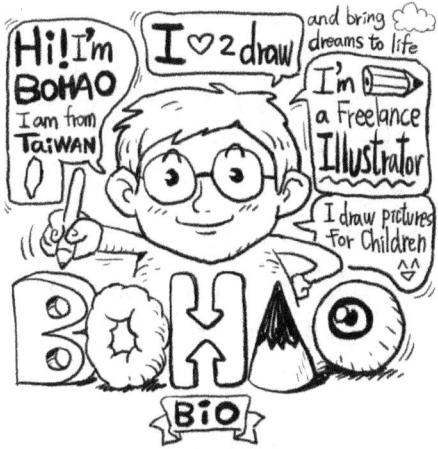

Bohao is a freelance illustrator who loves to draw and bring dreams to life.

He lives in a small town called Taichung just outside of Taipei, Taiwan. He graduated from the National Taichung University of Science and Technology in 2006, where he majored in Graphic Design. After working for several years for a small advertising agency, he became frustrated by the limitations of the job and decided to make a living as a freelance artist and drawing what he wanted to draw.

Bohao now dedicates his time to illustration projects that he enjoys and has illustrated several books and magazines.

In his free time, he loves watching anime and reading comics!

www.doghaveitday.wixsite.com/haopic

Recommended Resources

The Auspicious Arts Incubator was born in 2007. We are an arts business incubator dedicated to helping you build sustainable creative businesses by giving you the confidence along with the business and marketing skills necessary to thrive in a competitive marketplace. We work with independent artists and small & medium arts organizations in Australia, Canada and the USA.

We have developed some programs that will help you get further faster.

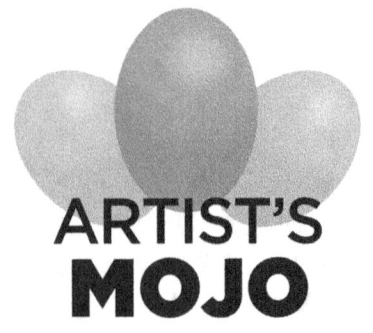

ARTIST'S MOJO

You are an awesome powerful artist... sometimes...

Get out of your own way.

If you have limiting beliefs, would like to have more self-confidence, and work smarter rather than harder, this 5-week course is for you.

What *you* get:

✓ *5 video modules, to be studied at your own pace*

✓ *Three 90-min one-on-one interactive sessions (in person or via web)*

✓ *Hardcover Mojo journal sketchbook*

RECOMMENDED RESOURCES

Module 1: **INTRODUCTION TO YOUR MOJO**

- *6 tested and proven activities that develop your Mojo*
- *Establishing dialogue with your Mojo*

Module 2: **BELIEF**

- *Everything you need to know about your limiting beliefs and how to change them NOW.*
- *Personal 90-min 1:1 Psych-K session*

Module 3: **CONFIDENCE**

- *Developing what it takes for an artist to gain confidence*
- *Personal 90-min 1:1 NLP session*

Module 4: **PEAK PERFORMANCE**

- *Specialised activities to develop your full range of skills to work smarter.*
- *Personal 90-min 1:1 performance coaching session*

Module 5: **INDUCTION**

- *Conscious and subconscious integration*
- *Installing your Mojo into your subconscious operating system.*

If you are really serious about making it.

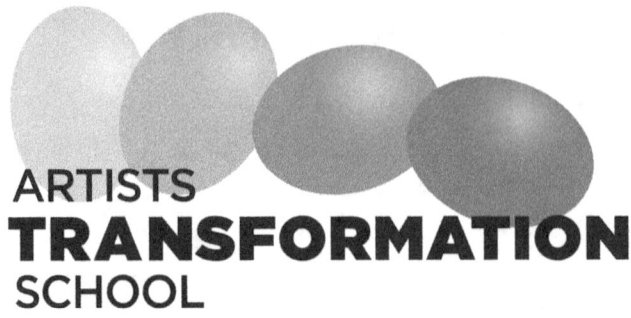

ARTISTS
TRANSFORMATION
SCHOOL

Transform yourself and your arts practice with our help.

To take the work of this book further, contact us about the Artists Transformation School. Our successful, signature incubation process is delivered live and on-line in 12 weeks with 9 more months of support and mentorship.

What you get:

Structured 12-module course with over 40 hours of video content, exercises and downloadable resources

- ✓ *Networking and peer support*
- ✓ *One-on-one coaching sessions*
- ✓ *Live on-line forums*
- ✓ *Website assessment*
- ✓ *Editing of your marketing copy*
- ✓ *Quick, ad-hoc coaching help*
- ✓ *2$^{1}/_{2}$-day live intensive workshop*
- ✓ *Post-course monthly modules*
- ✓ *ASAP membership*

Enrollment is limited, and artists are accepted by interview only.

RECOMMENDED RESOURCES

Module 1: **FOCUS** – *All the things you have on the go come into balance, so that you invest your time and energy in the things that will make money.*

Module 2: **BRANDING** – *Build your self-confidence and create work that is immediately successful, because you know why your fans and customers love you and your art.*

Module 3: **BELIEFS** – *Understand the neuroscience of your artist's brain to erase limiting beliefs, and change your emotional state now.*

Module 4: **GETTING IT RIGHT** – *Get the best team to support you, and create the right business structure from the start.*

Module 5: **GOALS & PLANNING** – *Create, write, and reach your goals so that you realize your potential.*

Module 6: **FINANCE** – *Become confident working with the 'money stuff' so knowing your numbers becomes easy and helpful.*

Module 7: **IT'S YOUR TIME** – *Develop new habits of time management, become more productive, and reduce stress.*

Module 8: **UNDERSTANDING YOU** – *Achieve greatness by using language that draws people and resources to you and your art.*

Module 9: **VALUE BASED LANGUAGE** – *Achieve greatness by using language that draws people and resources to you and your art.*

Module 10: **E-MARKETING** – *Have others market for you, because you've educated your fans and built strong relationships.*

Module 11: **SOCIAL MEDIA** – *Learn to use social media platforms effectively to build a community of support.*

Module 12: **GETTING THE MONEY** – *Succeed in getting the money you need to realise your goals.*

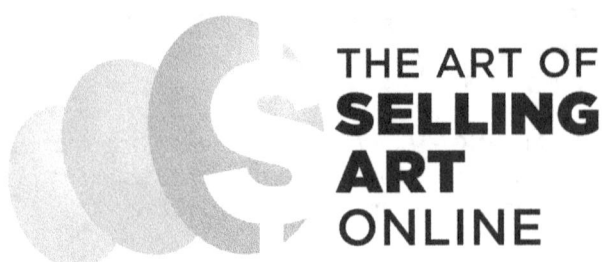

THE ART OF SELLING ART ONLINE

It's time to develop your online business and generate more sales than ever.

The online side of your business is the key to supporting you financially and leaving you enough time to work on your art without the stress of finding more customers.

THE ART OF SELLING ART ONLINE *is an easy six-month program of weekly modules with quick practical actions and monthly forums that will build your web business and help you reach more people.*

This course will:

- *fill in the gaps in the foundation of the online part of your arts business*

- *instruct you on how to build a results-oriented online marketing plan*

- *assist you in choosing the right products that customers actually want to buy*

- *show you how to optimize your website for sales*

- *and finally, teach you how to build that automated sales funnel that keeps customers coming and guides them towards making a sale.*

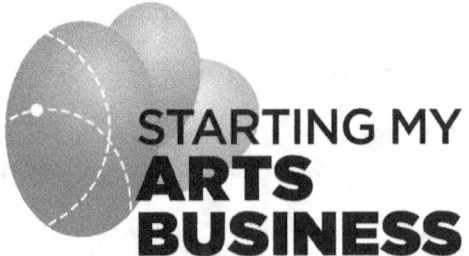

STARTING MY ARTS BUSINESS

It's hard to know where to start.

STARTING MY ARTS BUSINESS *is a self-directed short course of 4 modules with a total of 16 lessons created by artists for artists to help you take the correct first steps to get serious about your art as your business.*

If you only need a bit of help

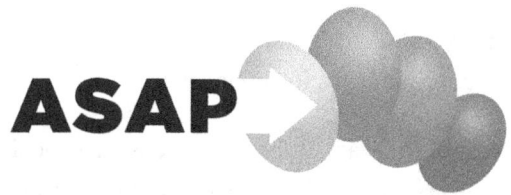

Stay on track and make steady progress on building your arts business.

The Auspicious Successful Artists Program (ASAP) is an exclusive membership site for artists with weekly and monthly tips, advice, and constant interaction between members.

Get access to tailor-made content, designed to help artists sell more art and make steady progress and be part of a community of like-minded professionals who want their art to be more than just a 'hobby'.

- *Each week you will be able to access members-only, exclusive, extended Hot tips and advice for artists on how to master your art and your life and build your business.*

- *Log in from anywhere and watch special interviews with guest experts and participate in live Q&As*

- *Connect to a community of artists, where you can reach out for help not only from us, but also from others who are going through the same things you are.*

- *Download e-books created specifically for challenges you are facing.*

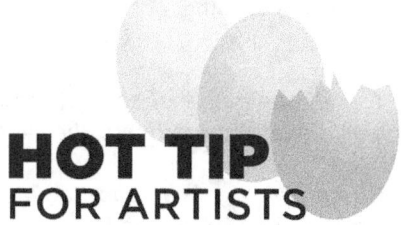

Five minutes of support every week.

Every week we release a short video with a practical tip to help you succeed. Sign up to get the weekly Hot Tip for Artists video delivered directly to your inbox. Plus, get access to the back catalogue of tips that have been helping artists make it in business.

But wait there's more!

Over the years we've worked with two amazing coaches, who help artists sort out limiting beliefs and develop confidence.

Liz O'Brien is part of the team at the Auspicious Arts Incubator. She is our Belief Buster. Liz uses PSYCH-K® as an integral part of helping artists let go of limiting beliefs that hold them back. What's really amazing about her work is that it is so fast and lasting. And the really cool thing is you can work with her from anywhere in the world over video conference or phone.

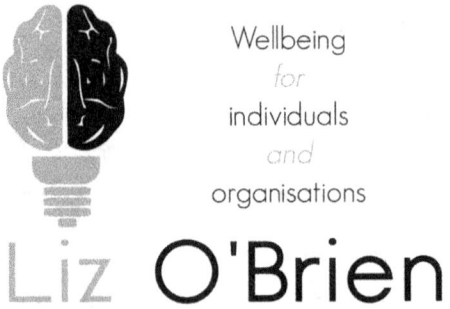

Wellbeing
for
individuals
and
organisations

Liz O'Brien

"The secret of life is BELIEF.
Rather than genes, it is our beliefs that control our lives.
PSYCH-K is a set of simple, self-empowering techniques that change your beliefs and your perceptions that impact your life at a cellular level."

– Bruce Lipton
PH. D Cellular Biologist, author of *"The Biology of Belief"*

Limiting beliefs are usually the cause of self-sabotaging behaviour that trips us up and stops us moving forward into the lives we want.

Using PSYCH-K ®, you can let go of self-sabotaging beliefs quickly and easily and live your life with more ease and joy.

Check out her website: **http://lizobrien.com.au**

or drop her an email: **liz@lizobrien.com.au**

Julie-Anne Black ('Jewells' to her friends) is also part of the team at the Auspicious Arts Incubator. She is our producer of Bold and Irresistible Communicators. Jewells' work is based in NLP (Neuro-Linguistic Programming). Her highly tuned intuitive sense combines with her years of helping artists be their very best selves. This combination means that whatever is holding you back, no matter what it is...she can help you identify it, figure it out, and change it.

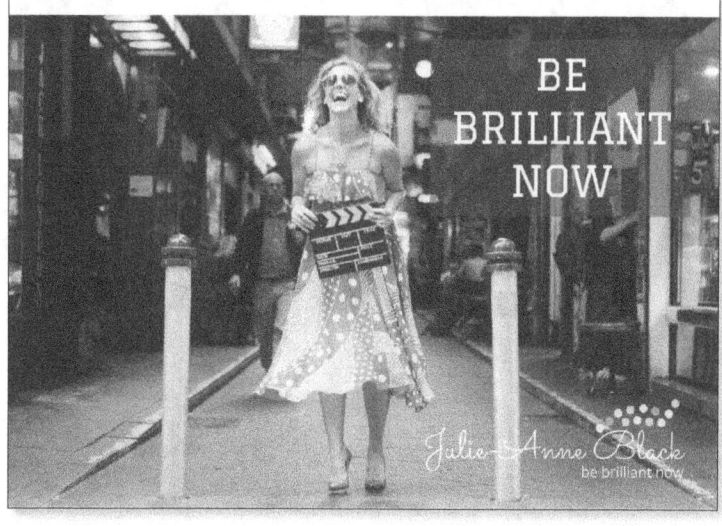